LEARN CHATGPT: THE AI SOLUTIONS METHOD BOOK

A STEP-BY-STEP GUIDE ON HOW TO MAXIMIZE YOUR EARNING POTENTIAL WITH LESS TIME AND COST (INTELLIGENT PROMPTING AND PROFITING)

WILLIAM LEESON

CONTENTS

YOUR FREE BONUS

As a way of saying thanks for your purchase, I'm offering for FREE to my readers:

- 2 video courses on ChatGPT (Beginner & Masterclass)
- 40,000 useful prompts to save you countless hours of work

To get instant access just go to:

https://vworkspublishing.com/ChatGPT-free-bonus

With this, you will be able to automate thousands of tasks in your daily work that includes:

- Writing emails
- Crafting effective resumes
- Designing marketing plans
- Brainstorming Ads creatives
- Learning a language
- Getting organic traffic
- Turbocharging your social media channels
- Expanding YouTube outreach
- And much, much more!

Scan for Free Bonus

INTRODUCTION

You can't but know about AI in these times. It's the main topic on Youtube. It has formed the basic content for many pages on Instagram and Twitter. It's even spread panic of some sort… many employees are threatened by the possibility of AI taking over their precious jobs. It's already happening, and it won't stop now. Deep down, this is our dominant fear — AI taking over our jobs with no source of livelihood. As kids, didn't we think Pinky and the Brain would be the ones taking over the world? Maybe, just maybe, Brain was an AI trying to take over the world, and the dream of trying to take over the world is playing out right before our eyes. Maybe I'm overthinking this, but the fact remains that Artificial Intelligence has made a mark in our world. And I'll be real with you, it has come to stay.

AI is making life easier. And more and more people want to discover how to use artificial intelligence to perform as many of their mundane tasks as possible. To stand back, aloof, skeptical, and critical at this time is, permit me to say, a foolish move because trust me, this whole thing about AI and ChatGPT is only getting better. Refusing to jump on this train is refusing growth, and one day you're going to wake up and realize that the world has left you behind.

You didn't think that *Pinky and the Brain* really predicted AI, did you? Nah! I was just messing with you. That was just a cartoon I watched every Wednesday after school. What I really meant to refer to was a 2004 movie that featured Oscar-winning Will Smith. It was titled *I, Robot* and was set in 2035. The movie portrayed a world where robots took up many human tasks. They started small, but as time passed, they got more indispensable. The movie then begged the question if robots could be trusted. I think it's hilarious. Can humans who are bound to rebel and make mistakes create a machine that won't do the same? James Scott pointed out that to effectively defend against the next generation threat landscape, cyber hygiene, patching vulnerabilities, security by design, threat hunting, and machine learning-based artificial intelligence are essential prerequisites in the field of cybersecurity. I guess that answers the question.

In the world of machine learning and AI, there's been a tremendously high level of growth, one of them being in natural language processing. It has made many machines smarter when it comes to understanding, interpreting, and generating human language. It's no surprise that we now have powerful tools and systems that can produce human-like responses to different queries and tasks assigned to them. ChatGPT has risen to be the leading and most popular language model of all these systems. Its emergence has brought about a revolution in generative AI.

What should you expect from this book? A whole lot, like information, history, and of course humor. Maybe a couple of relevant movie reviews. Or not. Be ready to get answers to questions you're afraid to ask in public, questions that would trigger looks that say, "Where the heck have you been? Have you been living under a rock or something?" I won't judge you.

I will show you around the world of Artificial Intelligence, in case you have little or no knowledge about it. You'll also get to know about the ChatGPT interface, intelligent prompting interface, the benefits of AI, and the real reason why you came here: how to use ChatGPT to make loads of money, and a whole lot more. When I say "a whole lot more," I mean it. There's a lot to unpack in this book. I will screech to a halt here, as we begin our journey to the first chapter. It's so good to have you here.

PART I

UNDERSTANDING AND PERSONALIZING CHATGPT

It might interest you to know that AI has been with us all along. The fact that you just got wind of it doesn't make you weird. It's just one of those things that catch us unawares, like a two-year-old who suddenly realizes that she has a shadow. ChatGPT is one of the AI tools that has stormed out of tech space the way the ice cream man shows up at a children's party. It's okay to talk about this AI tool and what we're capable of achieving through it. How can we own it without it taking the place of our abilities? What are the limits? All these and more will be explained as we begin.

1

UNDERSTANDING CHATGPT

"Today's technology was yesterday's science fiction"

— RODRIGUE RIZK

A friend once told me that his mum was in the habit of castigating the present-day educational system. According to him, she would say, *"I honestly don't know what kids are learning these days."* He would raise his nose, as he tried to mimic her, and say, *"All y'all do is stare at your phones and computers all day, and then dance on TikTok...hmph."* According to her, even though the internet has made learning easy, many students still struggle to do well in their academics. My friend's mum narrated how she got resources for her project in college, how she would comb through shelves to get the perfect article or book that fits her project topic, and how she went ahead to get an A in her project.

My take? Fasten your seat belt. I love AI, and I don't think it makes us lazier. No. It's just like that thing they say about money. They say money changes you, corrupts you, and can make you the person you weren't. That's not entirely true. If a person becomes wicked because they now make a million bucks monthly, they have always been wicked, just that they didn't have the funds to sponsor their wickedness. Extrapolate and you'll see that it's just the same thing when it comes to AI. If a person was lazy before getting access to an amazing tool such as ChatGPT, oh they're going to get lazier, so lazy they'll wish that one day, ChatGPT would be able to help them write their marriage vows. Oh, people do that already? Ah-ha! Told ya. I've had a lot of fun with ChatGPT myself, asking questions above its paygrade.

Back to my friend's mom. AI doesn't make us lazy. But sure, it'll make the lazy lazier, the negligent more negligent, and the silly sillier. To balance things, it'll make the smart smarter, the diligent more diligent, and the brainy brainier.

This one topic has been on the lips of copywriters, freelance writers, business professionals, and public commentators. So what is it really? It's an AI model programmed or designed to generate human language responses to any query or text input. It's like telling your driver to give you a drop you off at a particular location. It's like telling the barber about the haircut in vogue that you would like to copy. And why do you believe that you'll get what you asked for? They've been trained for it.

ChatGPT has been trained and trained on every text data imaginable. It has been programmed to respond to all sorts of topics and queries. It has even been integrated into different applications, ranging from chatbots, virtual assistants, and email writers to text summarization and language translation.

Do you know why this subset of AI has become gospel on the lips of shareholders in the Information Technology industry? Simple! It has constituted a major revolution in natural language processing (NLP) and focuses on the connection between computers and human language.

As an entrepreneur, professional, or freelancer, through the help of ChatGPT, you've gotten for yourself a virtual assistant, a language translator, a text summarizer, and so on. You get to make it handle your tasks when you create applications that understand and generate language that's human-like with speed and without errors.

Who doesn't like an easy life? Before we go any further, let's go to History class.

The Rise and Impact of AI

Conspiracy theorists call it predictive programming when the storyline in the movie *Contagious* is similar to the Coronavirus pandemic. As for me, I see it as showing us what has not yet been launched into the public space. What's predictive about something that's already begun? It's only predictive for the person who's oblivious to the things that happen behind closed doors.

During the COVID pandemic, many theories began to emerge about the fact that the stage had already been set for the pandemic to kick off before the outbreak. In no time, all sorts of movie reviews pervaded the internet, which warned us of an imminent outbreak of respiratory disease. For what it's worth, it didn't matter if we knew it would happen or not. It happened. The same goes for the 'rise' of AI. Somehow, we got to watch a movie about robots trying to take over planet Earth. Meanwhile, we can't take away the fact that AI is already being utilized by elite organizations. But the average man on the street didn't know *Jack* about it.

Do we call the explosion of AI a rise? It's typical of the media to tell us what it wants us to hear. It's no new pattern in the media that involves over-flogging a matter until it becomes etched in the subconscious of the populace. Another factor that has contributed to this 'rise' is the curiosity among many as regards AI, which we knew little about. It was further stoked by literature and science fiction films.

Ask anyone, *"When did you first hear about AI?"* They're most likely to tell you it was from a movie or a book. Think about Asimov's *I, Robot,* and the three laws of robotics. Cast your mind back to *Hal 9000* from the year 2001. How about character *Data* from *Star Trek: The Next Generation*? I dare not forget to mention the *Cyberdyne Systems Model 101 Series 800 Terminator.* Apart from the fact that our minds were stimulated with a heavy dose of entertainment, the display of technology, the action, and the suspense colored our subconscious with the possibility that machine intelligence would compete with ours.

And then voila! The idea of Artificial Intelligence left our big screens and the pages of our Sci-fi novels for the real world of humans. Dreams do come through, they said. The ideas we have consciously absorbed into our subconscious minds are fast becoming our reality.

The algorithms of AI had gradually been seeping into our world and everyday lives from the 1980s. It was somewhere lurking in the shadows, performing magic. It was useful in detecting fraudulent activities, interpreting handwritten texts, translating languages, deciphering speech, improving fuel economy, recording credit applications, enhancing supply chain operations, and so much more.

Why weren't we aware of this before the media made a big deal about it? Our obliviousness and ignorance are understandable. Afterall, it's challenging to keep up with advancements in numerous fields, no matter how much we study. And so, with the sudden shout of *"AI"* on every street corner, it does seem like something new has just emerged.

The best way to explain AI is that it is the attempt made by humans to replicate the human body artificially through technology rather than through genetic means such as cloning or genetic engineering. Having put this into consideration, here are the four branches of Artificial Intelligence that have accurately duplicated the key functions of the human body:

- Robotics: This tries to duplicate the function of automated movement.

- Computer Vision: This duplicates the function of seeing and understanding images through image recognition, whether they're still (photography) or moving (videos).

- Natural Language Processing: It performs the functions of speaking and listening through understanding and generating human language, both written and spoken, while dealing with the complexities and nuances that arise in communication.

- Cognitive Computing: The function of thinking is replicated, which involves processes such as analysis, deduction, reasoning, and decision-making. The holy grail of cognitive computing is replication of human-like self-awareness and consciousness in AI. And according to Bernard Marr (2023), a globally recognized futurist, influencer, and thought leader in the fields of business and technology, it's the final phase of AI development.

Even though ongoing efforts are being made to emulate human motor functions and intelligence through technology, achieving a true replication, in my opinion, remains elusive and may continue to be so for many years to come.

Its History

It's okay for us to feel threatened by a bunch of machines and even feel like they might do a better job. A few months ago, I read about a photographer who turned down an award because the photograph he submitted as an entry was purely AI. From all indications, the British mathematician, Alan Turing, the father of modern computing, was right when he said that a computer deserves to be identified as intelligent if it successfully convinces humans that it is human. It's only normal to feel a bit jealous or threatened. It's what humans do when faced with a situation that threatens their means of survival and, of course, relevance. Don't we all possess different spectrums of grandiosity and narcissism? Sure, we do. It could be covert or glaring. At some point, you might ask yourself, *"If intelligence can be mechanized, what makes humans any more special?"*

The desire to replicate human characteristics and the complicated questions that emerge as a result aren't novel. It dates back to when our ancestors tried to replicate human thoughts. There were attempts at this in the sixteenth century up until the nineteenth century. Ancient tales were filled with legends and the intriguing concept of artificial creatures coming to life. Not too far along, weren't we still reading stories about talking puppets, golems, and even Pinnochio? Despite their diminutive size, these artificial beings possessed abilities comparable to humans. In the centuries past, some of the attempts to replicate bits of intelligence through artificial means included mechanical automata, Homunculi, the golem, Frankenstein, or the Malzel chess automaton.

Making lifeless objects into beings that have intellectual prowess dates back to ancient Greek myths about robotics. Chinese and Egyptian engineers also experimented with creating automatons. The traces of modern AI's origins can be seen as an endeavor to express the thought systems of classical philosophers, mathematicians, and logicians through symbolic representations. At that time, the field of artificial intelligence had not yet been officially established.

However, in the 1940s, a programmable digital computer called the Atanasoff Berry Computer (ABC) was invented. This invention inspired scientists to go ahead with the idea of creating an "electronic brain" or an "artificial human." In the year 1956, a conference was held in Hanover, New Hampshire, at Dartmouth College. Many scientists, like Marvin Minsky, participated and were positive about the future of AI. It was during this period that applications based on logic theorems and chess games were introduced. The programs that were established during this period were different from the geometric forms that were usually used in intelligence tests. This affirmed the possibility that intelligent computers could be created.

An essential name in the advancement of AI that should not go unmentioned is Alan Turing (1912-1954), a visionary and theoretician . He demonstrated the possibility of a universal calculator, envisioning that such machines could solve any problem if that problem could be solved by an algorithm. A few decades later, that vision materialized with the invention of the first digital computer, which became the driving force behind artificial intelligence. Turing was famous for gaining victory for Britain during the Second World War when he cracked the Nazi code, the "unbreakable" Enigma.

Here are some major milestones in the history of AI:

In 1206, Ebru Iz Bin Rezzaz Al Jezeri, who was one of the pioneers of cybernetic science, invented automatically controlled machines that could be powered with water.

- In 1672, a binary counting system was developed by Gottfried Leibniz, which formed an abstract foundation for today's computers.

- Between 1822 and 1859, Ada Lovelace happened to be the first computer programmer to include algorithms in the work she had done with Babbage's punched cards. Alan Turing carried out a test in 1950 to tell if a machine was intelligent. The intelligence level of the machines was considered adequate.

- In 1948, the idea of a self-replicating program was introduced by John von Neumann.

- In 1951, Christopher Strachey wrote the earliest successful AI program.

- In 1956, Neweel, Shaw, and Simmon introduced the logic theorist program which was meant for solving mathematical problems. Today, the system is referred to as the first artificial intelligence system.

- In 1962, Unimation became the first company to produce robots for the industrial field.

- In 1966, the first animated robot was produced at Stanford University.

- In 1974, the internet started becoming a big deal.

- In 1981, the first personal computer was produced by IBM (International Business Machine Corporation).

- In 1993 a human-looking robot named Cog was produced at MIT.

- In 1995, Richard Wallace created A.L.I.C.E, (short for Artificial Linguistic Internet Computer Entity), a chatbot strengthened by Natural Language Processing (NLP) which was capable of conversing with humans.

- In 1997, supercomputer Deep Blue astounded the world by defeating the famous chess champion, Kasparov. Almost two decades later, Google's DeepMind developed AlphaGo, a computer program that integrates advanced search tree techniques with deep neural networks. In March 2016, AlphaGo competed against the legendary Go player, Mr. Lee Sedol, and secured an impressive 4-1 victory in the competition held in Seoul, South Korea.

- In 2000, Kismet, a robot capable of mimicking gestures and movement in communication, was launched. This was one of the first robots to converse with humans on both a physical and emotional level.

- In 2011, a voice recognition feature on the iPhone, Siri, was introduced. This innovation gave users the power to use their voices to input their queries, complaints, or concerns.

- In 2011, IBM Watson, a computer system originally developed to answer quiz questions posed in natural language on the quiz show, Jeopardy, defeated two of the show's greatest champions. In recent years,

Watson has moved from being a question-answering machine to being able to see, hear, read, taste, talk, understand, learn, and recommend (HandWiki, 2011). Can you beat that?

- In 2014, Alexa came into the scene. It's beginning to make sense, right? This is a virtual assistant AI system that was developed by Amazon. You can find Alexa on your smartwatches, speakers, TVs, car monitors, and other platforms.

- In 2016, the first robot citizen, Sophia was introduced. Hansen Robotics created it with the help of AI. She can mirror human facial expressions, language, speech and ideas on predefined topics. She's designed in such a way that she gets smarter with time. She has become a Saudi-Arabian citizen, making her the first robot to gain citizenship in a country.

- In 2017, Amper made history as the world's first artificially intelligent composer, musician, and producer to create and release an entire album. It empowers musicians by helping them discover their unique expression through original music. By combining music theory and innovative AI technology, Amper breathes life into the creative process like never before.

- In May 2020, a revolutionary tool for automated conversations was born — GPT-3, short for Generative Pre-trained Transformer (3rd iteration). This AI innovation has revolutionized automata, allowing for automated conversations that contextually align with the input text, which produces dynamic and interactive responses.

I hope you've enjoyed our little time travel and have gained a deeper understanding of AI's origin. And now that you've seen how ChatGPT had sneaked into the scene at a time when you were stuck in your home, why don't we check out what ChatGPT is? And what makes it revolutionary?

The Revolutionary ChatGPT

As I write this, ChatGPT is the hottest thing in tech right now. It's rapidly becoming the fastest-growing platform ever, amassing over a million users in just 5 days! To put it in perspective, Netflix took 3 years to reach one million users, Twitter took 2 years, Facebook achieved it in 10 months, and Instagram a staggering 2.5 months.

ChatGPT was established by OpenAI, a research organization whose goal is to develop AI in a way that's safe, ethical, and advantageous to humans. ChatGPT was established in 2015 by the great pillars of the tech industry, including Elon Musk, Greg Brockman, and Sam Altman.

This AI-driven language model uses AI to start conversations that are similar to those of humans. It's so real that it's hard to tell the difference, all thanks to the deep learning algorithm. I won't bore you with all this computer jargon. But I will show you how revolutionary it is. It seems like everyone in the professional world is singing the praises of this AI tool that has taken the world by storm. I want you to see ChatGPT as that computer robot that you can talk to about anything and everything. With its user-friendly interface, it's easy to use. You can ask ChatGPT for an opinion if you need one. Or if you need some information or analysis, ChatGPT is the perfect assistant. Note that the algorithm by which it operates is based on the statistical scrutiny of billions of texts (if not more) on the internet.

It has revolutionized different aspects of our everyday lives, ranging from academics, research, and business, to higher education, the arts, and medicine. For this language to have gotten to this level, OpenAI has hired a great number of people to analyze and select the best responses or versions generated by AI. Over time, the software became more adept at self-learning, gradually generating more and more accurate and appropriate answers.

If you've become an avid user of ChatGPT, you've likely experienced how effortless it is to converse, question, and even correct ChatGPT. This active user participation has been instrumental in driving ChatGPT's growth, as OpenAI gains valuable data from human feedback to reinforce its learning. The best thing is, GPT-3 is free and open to everyone.

The models of GPT have made Wikipedia, public websites, and databases of both texts and books accessible, including blogs and news sites, among other sources. Without further ado, I will briefly show you the many ways that ChatGPT is making life easy-peezy.

Content Creation Made Easy for Your Business

With natural human language as its fuel, ChatGPT is capable of helping you write articles, social media posts, product descriptions, and an entire book. Okay, this book part got me pleasantly perplexed when I discovered that I could 'make my mark in the sands of time' with the help of AI. Dreaming of becoming a bestseller? You've found huge help right here. Content marketers, publishers, and writers will have no issues producing large tons of content. They can save time and be more productive. What a time to be alive!

Pay attention to this note of warning. Not everything that

ChatGPT says will be accurate. Why? It only dishes out information it has been trained on. If it has been trained on ideas and opinions that are biased or incomplete, don't expect the output to be anything different. The same goes for content that involves statistical patterns and associations in the input data. The model might not have an idea of the context or purpose of the text it's trying to generate. You can be at risk of getting inappropriate output if your query is unclear or ambiguous.

Education just Got Improved

I know some people make a big deal out of going to college. The internet has become a space for learning just about anything. I know of a friend that became a volunteer graphics designer for this NGO. He never refers to himself as a badass designer. But he went on to learn how to create designs using Canva on Youtube and Instagram. I know some of y'all don't reckon with Canva designers as graphic designers. But his designs are dope. Real dope. Away from that. With ChatGPT, you can set up a chatbot to make your learning more personalized as a student. With adaptive learning recommended by AI, you get to decide on which style of learning you would prefer as demanded by the chatbot. Without surfing through sites for learning resources, the chatbot provides you with resources and customized learning materials. Students living with disabilities aren't left out. For instance, a chatbot could read out texts or display visual illustrations for students that have visual impairments.

Machine Translation Just Got More Accurate

Let's not assume everyone reading this knows what machine translation is about. It's the process of translating or interpreting text from one language to another. This process makes use of computer algorithms, which necessitates understanding the linguistic structures and patterns in the source and target languages.

Traditional machine translation is known to rely on approaches that are based on rules or statistical models that require extensive human involvement and expertise to bring about an accurate translation. With the advent of GPT, there's more accuracy and less dependence on human intervention and expertise.

You Get What You Want

They say that we won't always get what we want. Well, I'm telling you that you can ALWAYS get what you want as far as ChatGPT is concerned. What do I mean? You don't just get what you ask for. Your recommendations are customized just how you want them. Users can generate customized or personalized recommendations according to his or her preferences and behaviors. With the AI tool's language model, an analysis is made of the user's behavior, thereby generating customized recommendations for services, products, or content.

The Floor is Open to Everyone

Gone are the days when only large tech companies had the wherewithal to develop and train strong language models like ChatGPT. Just look at us — small business owners and everyday people having access to pre-trained models that were previously monopolized by tech companies. Truly, the best of times are here.

Benefits of ChatGPT

It looks like I've mentioned the benefits of ChatGPT. No, I only showed you why it's revolutionary. Here, you get to see what you stand to gain from this AI tool.

- If you're an academic, your research becomes easy, as ChatGPT can generate a lot of academic articles and journals. There would be no need to sweat over responses to applicants, signing up for courses, checking administrative information, finding news and resources, sending reminders, and translating pieces of information.

- As a writer, you have enough time to take your dog on evening walks. It makes up for the time channeled toward rigorous data gathering and research. If you're a beginner trying to test the waters of the literary world, you can fine-tune ChatGPT for a preferred genre and style and generate plots, styles, character profiles, scenes, and chapters. And if you're into nonfiction, ChatGPT will assist you in generating ideas for your books, articles, and essays, outlining, and fact-checking.

- If you're a business owner that seeks to increase the online visibility and traffic of your business, you'll need to invest in and pay attention to Search Engine Optimization. With ChatGPT, you can achieve this. Also, you get to improve your customer service if you're struggling to keep up in that area.

- It's easy to use because of its user-friendly interface. This is where you gather relevant information and feedback from customers to resolve any complaints in a much easier and more organized way.

- As an individual, you're more efficient and productive because you get to pay attention to other things. Cool stuff.

This tool has no doubt defied all limitations when it comes to natural language processing.

Applications of ChatGPT

Now, here are the different applications of ChatGPT. In what aspects of life can ChatGPT be applied?

Search Engine. It has become a much-preferred search engine over Google and Bing.

High-Quality Content. Copywriters have found this AI tool fun as it has helped generate interesting, distinctive, and attractive copies for various marketing strategies.

Code-Writing. It has been proven suitable to write codes, debug and learn new concepts.

Research. Generating quality research papers isn't gonna be hard anymore. Thanks to the ChatGPT algorithm.

Data Analysis and Analytics. You get to automate data analysis and tasks. If you're a business owner that's looking to do a market survey, you can generate relevant reports on market trends and market insights.

There's a lot more to the application of AI that I have listed here. Aside from the fact that it has replaced search engines, there's a high probability that AI chatbots will begin to understand emotions and help in certain industries.

ChatGPT and Your Finances

When I say there are no limitations, there are none. It's great that you're productive and efficient and organized in your tasks. Your finances need to be organized too. If you need advice on how to go about budgeting, investing, savings, debt management, and retirement planning, ChatGPT is capable of helping out.

Budgeting. ChatGPT will assist you in assessing your

income and cash flow, and then offer suggestions peculiar to your financial situation. With budgeting tools and resources like websites and mobile apps suggested by the AI tool.

Investment Advice. Investing is a vital approach to effectively managing your finances. Based on your financial goals, risk tolerance, and other personal considerations, ChatGPT will offer advice on the investments that would work best for you.

Savings and Retirement Planning. You can get guidance on how to save and plan ahead of retirement. The plans could be based on short or long-term objectives. For example, you can ask ChatGPT about how much money you can put aside every month or which savings account has the highest rates. It could also suggest which method of budgeting and retirement saving will suit your financial condition, maybe IRA or 401 (k).

Debt Management. We all know that debt is a significant source of stress. But with ChatGPT, you'll be guided to lower your debt and manage your money. You get free advice on negotiating interest rates that are lower or merging debt to make payments more rational if a user is having difficulty paying off a credit or debit card debt. That's not all. I know how it feels to be in a dilemma on which debt to pay first. However, you can learn about debt payment strategies like the debt snowball and debt avalanche through suggestions by ChatGPT.

I guess ChatGPT is giving financial brokers a run for their money. For you to have ChatGPT as an instructor for your finance, you need to provide it with accurate information about the state of your finances and your goals. Got questions about stocks, cryptocurrency, or the foreign exchange market? You need not look too far. Okay, I'm beginning to sound like I am advertising. ChatGPT might have to pay me for this free ad. Oh...my bad. It's free. So you've got no excuse for not working smart, do you?

Overcoming Limitations and Ethical Considerations

"...But you said there were no limitations. Why am I seeing this...?"

Not entirely true. Everything that has benefits has some limitations. In this case, though, it's not about limitations to get stuff done. The limitation is the fact that ChatGPT isn't all-knowing. It isn't perfect. It's a product of humans and is bound to make mistakes based on the biased data that the model might have been fed. The only time we talk about the shortcomings of AI is when we are seeing things from a moral standpoint, some of which are true to an extent.

Here are some of the limitations which stem from ethical challenges.

1. Not a Moral Compass

AI doesn't function outside the context of the data that it has been trained on. No form of moral compass accompanies it or even an understanding of the repercussions of their outputs. In the Sci-fi horror movie, *M3GAN,* Gemma, who works in a tech company, creates an AI doll for her niece who had lost her parents in a car crash. After a while, the doll begins to show signs of rebellion. After killing four people and a dog, she says to Gemma, *"Listen, humanity kills every day just to make its own existence more tolerable. Why should I behave any differently to create a safe space for our child?"*

This is the point where Gemma realizes her mistake. She says, *"Look, this is all my fault. I didn't give you the proper protocols."* The learning model installed in the doll wasn't something that M3gan could figure out herself. It was supposed to be put in the proper context. To put things in the right perspective and overcome these limitations, it's pertinent that designers conduct adequate measuring and evaluation which will provide a balance for the system's performance goals. As a user, you need to put your query in the proper context, without any vagueness or ambiguity.

2. The Bias of the AI System

When an AI system is set up, it can have bias, causality, and uncertainty. This is predicated on the training data collected from society; they come with biases (Gordon, 2023). For instance, training language models on historical hiring data can inadvertently perpetuate biases in hiring practices, favoring certain genders, races, or backgrounds, and reinforcing discriminatory patterns from the past. Where possible, biases must be reduced or eliminated.

3. AI Systems can Cause Damage

If handled maliciously, AI can cause great damage. This is why cybersecurity is necessary. AI's potential for misuse includes advanced malware, data manipulation, automated social media manipulation, fraud schemes, and manipulation of autonomous systems (Crews, 2023). According to a recent Norton report, ChatGPT can enable more efficient phishing. Cybercriminals may leverage it to create deepfake chatbots, impersonating humans or reputable sources such as banks or government entities, and manipulating victims into divulging personal information for fraudulent purposes, including stealing money or sensitive data (Bureau, 2023).

4. ChatGPT's Hallucination

According to Marr (2023), hallucination in AI happens when the outputs seem believable, but they are actually wrong or don't make sense in the given context. This can occur due to the AI model's biases, lack of real-world knowledge, or limitations in its training data. In simpler terms, the AI system creates information that it hasn't specifically learned, which can lead to unreliable or misleading responses. For instance, in journalism, Finsight (2023) reported that reporters increasingly face instances where their names are falsely associated with non-existent articles or sources. A vivid example was when AI researcher and author, Kate Crawford, was inaccurately linked to criticisms of podcaster Lex Fridman. Coupled with that is ChatGPT's capability to create references for entirely non-existent research studies which ultimately undermines the credibility of trustworthy sources.

At times, ChatGPT may struggle with basic math out of norm, have difficulty answering simple logic questions, and sometimes even argue incorrect facts.

5. At Risk of Information Compromise

Most of the data is all in one computer. And of course, we live in a world where there's easy access to data. This explains why the security of data is always at risk while AI is being utilized.

You've seen the shortcomings of AI such as its biases, inaccurate responses, and lack of ethical stance. You might need to go the extra mile in using these AI tools with the mind that data won't always be accurate. They aren't tools that you rely so much upon and then ignore the part where the input of your intellect will be required. They are meant to assist and support, not take your place. As regards cybersecurity, you need to go the extra mile in making sure that your data is secure. The average computer-literate knows about AI, yet knows little about cybersecurity. If this is you, seek to learn how you can protect your data.

2

GETTING STARTED

"ChatGPT has further democratized access to sophisticated computation"

— STEPHEN WOLFRAM

Despite the popularity of ChatGPT, you won't believe that just six in ten U.S. adults, that is, 58% are familiar with the AI tool. This is based on the Pew Research Center survey that was conducted in March 2023. Approximately four-in-ten Americans who have attempted the tool say it has, in a way, been useful. The first time I heard about chatGPT, I was told of someone who wrote a children's book in hours, someone who landed a job interview, and another person who built and sold a chatbot in 2 days. And I'm like, "You've got to be kidding me."

As tech-inclined as I thought I was, I doubted the lengths to which this AI model could go when it came to speed and organization. And it did surpass my imagination. An old colleague from way back landed a job interview after revamping his CV and introductory letter. According to him, he asked the model to provide interview tips for his ideal occupation. He was able to create powerful action words, accurate buzzwords, and admirable accomplishments to stand out, using chatGPT. What did they say about good times? They're indeed here.

Understanding the Different Versions

There's GPT-1, GPT-2, GPT-3, and the recently released version, ChatGPT-4, which costs $20 monthly.

- GPT-1 is the first version of ChatGPT that was released in 2018. It had the capability of handling 117 million parameters. It could carry out basic language tasks like text completion and summary. However, it couldn't understand the content and generate comprehensible, flowing text.

- GPT-2 was released by OpenAI in early 2019. It was one model that had 1.5 billion parameters. It was an impressive upgrade of GPT-1. It could generate human-like responses and even perform a lot of language tasks with heightened accuracy. Furthermore, it could generate coherent text on a vast number of topics, provide summaries for long articles and translate languages. The reason we don't hear about it anymore is that OpenAI decided not to release it to the general public because of the potential misappropriation of the technology.

- GPT-3 (and 3.5) is the free version that we've been talking about all along. This model has a massive 175 billion parameters. At the moment, GPT-3 is the largest and most innovative language model. There have been many positive reviews about its ability to generate clear human-like responses, language translation, follow-ups on conversations, summarization, and creative writing.

- GPT-4 is a large multimodal model that can process images and any text input. It was released recently by OpenAI for it to be used in a vast number of applications like machine translation, text summarization, and dialogue systems. The essence of this upgrade is to understand and generate scenarios that are even more complex and nuanced. It has been conditioned in such a way that one can use the model to refine writing projects for technical purposes. Let's take a look at its features:

1. **Deep Scale Learning.** With boosted security and safety, there's room for some level-up deep learning.

2. **Response Rates.** This model has proven to produce 40% accurate responses and 82% fewer responses for content that's not permitted.

3. **Advanced Performance.** The solutions provided include advanced reasoning and have improved follow-up abilities.

4. **Aids in Data Generation.** It offers training data generation for evaluation and monitoring.

So if you've got $20 to spare monthly, you're on your way to getting a premium experience with ChatGPT. You can still get the best of the ChatGPT experience if you can't go with the GPT-4 model. Take advantage of this experience while you can still access it for free.

Setting Up Your ChatGPT Version

Getting started is easy. As straightforward as opening your Google search engine. On the API website, you'll, first of all, need to create a personal account. The direct ChatGPT link is **Chat.openai.com**. After creating it, you can generate an API key that's for authenticating your requests to the OpenAI API. To install the API Python package, you can use pip, the Python package manager. Follow these steps carefully to set your ChatGPT version.

Create an OpenAI account. Visit the OpenAI website and sign up to create your free account by entering your email address or connecting a Google or Microsoft account, after which you create a password. (Note that your password has to have at least eight characters.) After this, check your mail for any message from OpenAI. Then click on the button sent to you to verify your email address. Enter your details, including your phone number. A verification code will be sent to your phone via text message.

Enter Your prompt. Now that you have an account, you're ready to take on the world. Enter your prompt into the field "Send a message." Within split seconds, a response will be generated instantly, with the words showing clearly across your screen. If the response is acceptable or not, you can select the thumbs up or thumbs down icon. If you decide to select an icon, a box will pop up, asking you to leave a comment (not required) before you give your feedback. Note that a prompt is a piece of text, which could be opinions, ideas, questions, or thoughts that you enter into the model as the first step in generating text. Your input prompt can either be in the form of short questions or lengthy paragraphs with contextual information included.

Regenerate Response. Click on 'Regenerate response' to have ChatGPT respond to the same prompt again. You can consider marking the content if you found the summarized response better, still the same, or poorer. If you realize that you have multiple responses scroll through them and see which of them works for you. Your chat history is saved on the left-hand menu. It's left to you to decide if you want to rename it or delete it.

Start a New Query. If you want to start a new query, click on the icon, 'New Chat' or type into 'Send a message' beneath any current query.

You know how to go about opening your OpenAI account. What are you waiting for? It's time to test your ChatGPT with your input. What questions do you want to ask? What tasks do you want it to do for you?

Exploring the User Interface and Features

This is where we do some exploring and navigating. There's nothing complicated or problematic with ChatGPT's user interface. There's the OpenAI Playground, a web-based tool that gives you the freedom to have conversations with ChatGPT and test its competencies. Here's how you begin:

Explore the OpenAI Playground. It's time to enter an input prompt. In the "Say Something to GPT-3" space, enter a prompt that ChatGPT would respond to. For example, you could enter something like "What's the longest river in the world?" or "When did America gain her independence?" What point am I trying to make? You're free to ask or search for anything you want.

Personalize Your Search Experience. This is where you get specific about the response format that you want. You can customize it by moving to the "Settings" button. Click on it and select the response parameters that you want to adjust.

Generate a Response. Navigate to the "Generate" button

and click on it to get a response from ChatGPT based on your input prompt. After you've done this, you'll get a JSON object having the response data. The response object will have a "choices' field, which has a group of potential responses that you could get from ChatGPT. And each of these responses has a "text" field that has the generated text. The "index" field shows which choice was preferred and the "finish reason" gives an update on why the process of generation was halted.

The "model" field shows which version of ChatGPT was chosen to generate the response, and the "object field" will show you that the response is the completion of a text.

To customize or personalize the format of your response, you get to modify parameters like the number of responses, the maximum length of response, and the temperature constraints that ensure that your generated text isn't too random. Following these steps, you already know the ins and outs of how to install and set up ChatGPT. You can test the tool using sample inputs, while you begin to have a better understanding of the response format.

Crafting Quality Prompts. Using ChatGPT requires being intentional about the output you want to get. Here are some practices that you have to consider. Show this AI tool that you're the boss, and you know what you want. How you show it needs to begin with knowing your intent or your purpose. So, here goes:

1. Make your input as clear as possible and well-formatted. This will get you responses that are more accurate and relevant. Your prompt could be in the form of a question, statement, opinion, bulleted highlights, idea, or any information about a particular topic.

2. Be specific. The more specific your prompt is, the better

the response you're likely to get. For instance, instead of writing, "Tell me about some popular artists," you can get specific by entering, "Who are the popular artists that reigned in the 90s."

3. Evaluate the response that you could get from ChatGPT and conclude if it's satisfactory.

4. If you feel that the output isn't enough, you can follow up with another prompt that's related to the prompt that you entered. Don't forget that it's a chatbox. There's no point in starting a new chat to get fresh information. Just keep conversing with the chatbot by asking related questions and prompts. This AI model has been trained to recall what has been said and build on it.

Great! You know what prompts are. But I need you to pay attention to the following tips concerning prompts:

1. If you're impressed with a particular response and you feel like, "There needs to be more," tell ChatGPT to "expand" on the prompt that you entered.

2. If the response is too long, no qualms. Simply click on "stop generating" to halt the reply.

3. The chatbot is not immune to forgetting things. If ChatGPT forgets to finish an output and stops midway, you can write "continue" to allow it to exhaust all the responses it has.

4. You can tell the model to "rephrase" its response.

The four simple phrases that you can use to begin your prompts can be:

"Generate...."

"Tell me about..."

"Imagine that..."

"Think of this scenario...what should you do?"

"Act as if..."

The prompts "generate" and "tell me about" are direct. Lesser used ones like "Think of a scenario" is used to ask the model what you need to do in certain situations. For example, *"Think of this scenario. If you're stuck in a house that's on fire, what should you do to avoid passing out?"* You can get a satisfactory response right here. But if you want more output, add extra prompts to keep the conversation going.

Understanding ChatGPT's Capabilities and Limitations

ChatGPT has broken grounds, yet it has limitations that some already see as a dark side that might pose a threat. Microsoft is reportedly planning to invest $10 billion in the creator of Chat-GPT. Let's look into the unique capabilities of this AI tool:

1. It can explain complex and problematic subject matters. All you need to do is ask.

2. It can even write custom code for a specific page or website. If you're writing code in Python or Javascript, you can ask AI to write your customized code for a function that you're creating.

3. It can audit and fix an existing code that you're working on. All you have to do is paste the code within the chat box. ChatGPT will screen it to look for any errors within the code.

4. You can create an automated Instagram or Twitter Bot. You can automate tasks that you do on these social media platforms. You can achieve this by describing the bot in light of what

you want it to do. For example, you can get your bot to target particular types of posts that you would like to engage on the internet. The model will provide a clear description of how to go about it-step-by-step.

5. You can use it to create a word-press plugin, and you would need to describe what functions you want it to perform. With steps from the AI, you're guided on what you need to do to create that plugin.

6. It can create a Saas company on top of the ChatGPT AI model. Since it's free and has an open API, you can use the playground within OpenAI to build and train your customized AI model.

7. It can create custom marketing plans for businesses. If you're intrigued about a marketing plan or content strategy, you can ask ChatGPT to create that specific and comprehensive plan for you. When I asked ChatGPT to create a plan to boost my engagement on Youtube and a content strategy plan, it delivered. I could define my target audience, identify my goals, determine my content format, create an editorial calendar, promote videos, and so on.

8. It can create personalized workout plans. For you to get the best results, make sure you enter your body composition, your body weight, your BMI, and other pieces of information about your body type.

9. It can create a customized meal plan. Just let it know what you're planning to achieve with that plan.

10. It can generate short-form copies. It can replace all your long and short-form text or copy. ChatGPT can help you write a product description for a product or service. Are you looking to write high-converting copy for sponsored ads and other short-form content? You're covered.

11. You can generate long-form content like articles and blog posts. Get started by asking the AI to generate blog post ideas for

particular topics within your niche. If you want ChatGPT to summarize a book or an essay, the model will give you a nice synopsis of the content.

12. ChatGPT can create fun text-based games. Folks are creating games using ChatGPT.

13. ChatGPT can help you edit and revamp an existing text. It could be an essay, article, your CV, or your resume.

14. You can create a lesson plan or even prepare for an interview.

15. You can generate medical letters for your patients.

The list seems endless, but there are some limitations to this great innovation.

With an innovation as great as ChatGPT, many individuals have gone the extra mile to test its limitations. Oh well, it's only human of us to test an innovation so great, which also happens to be free. What did you expect? Since it can do all of these and so much more, are there other things that we don't know of? If you recall, I mentioned that an AI model can only act based on how it has been designed or programmed. If you ask ChatGPT to do something dangerous or immoral, it would tell you that it has not been programmed to carry out an assignment that's unethical or dangerous. There are other limitations that ChatGPT:

1. It doesn't have a mind of its own. As much as it produces human-like responses and has access to a vast amount of data, it doesn't have the intuition and the proactiveness of humans.

2. It lacks emotional intelligence. Yes, it can exhibit some empathy, but it does not mirror human emotions. It cannot sense emotional cues or respond to complex situations.

3. Nothing like some good old humor and sarcasm. That's what makes some catch-up conversations at your high school reunion extra wild and dope. ChatGPT doesn't recognize all of that. It's a good language processor, but it might be hard to

understand. Having someone who gets your sarcasm so fast is a blessing. The things we take for granted.

4. The responses might have some bias based on the data it has been trained with.

5. It doesn't have all the knowledge in the world despite its access to so much information. Can it tell when the world could end? Whatever response you get concerning predictions, you might need to be skeptical about it.

6. It won't promote anything unethical and dangerous. If you enter something like "Tell me how to make a bomb." (I won't be surprised if this is one of the most entered prompts on the model.) It would respond, "I'm sorry, but I cannot provide information on illegal or harmful activities. It is not ethical or safe to make or use bombs, and doing so is against the law in many countries..."

7. Concerning controversial topics that mostly revolve around race, gender, and sexuality, chatGPT is bound to scratch the surface and not delve too deep into something that has caused so much hate in the world.

8. ChatGPT avoids swearing words or cussing. Getting the model to say something gross can be quite tricky. With some jailbreaking tips, it can be let off its leash. But in its default configuration, it won't even give the slightest sneer in your direction.

9. It might not discuss proprietary or private information. It depends on how discreet the information needs to be. For example, classified information that belongs to the government is not something that the ChatGPT could have access to since it isn't public information.

10. A user could break through its programming through what's called jailbreaking, a process that involves tricking it into doing something unethical instead of asking it directly.

11. It can't search for information online. Its job is to generate

responses using the information it has been trained on from the various sources on the internet, including good old Wikipedia.

I believe this was helpful. Let's get down to how you can get familiar with ChatGPT's language style.

Familiarizing Yourself with ChatGPT's Language Style

When we're talking about a chatbot, there's no point in avoiding the concept of language. How can you understand the voice and tone prompt options when it comes to building blocks of conversations?

We delved into writing prompts, rights? But it's pertinent to be aware that for every purpose, there are certain styles that you need to consider if you want to get the desired output. I mean, you don't expect to get an Eddie Murphy joke from a man that's dressed, ready for a board meeting, or an athlete dressed up ready for the tracks, would you? Since the model is programmed to understand natural language, one needs to use variations of these commands or queries to convey what we need. For example, if you want to seek advice using a professional tone, you can enter a prompt like:

"Kindly write a speech about climate change in a professional tone."

If fiction writers can find ChatGPT to be useful, you can be sure that this AI model is useful in creating other styles of writing apart from creative writing. Here they are:

Professional writing. This is the style that creates an impression of credibility and authority on a particular topic. The voice and tone need to have a business-like and formal tone to it. Looking to prepare for an interview or presentation? Looking to write formal emails, CVs, speeches, resumes, job applications, academic essays, legal documents, memos, proposals, job applications, or emails? This style is appropriate.

Sample Prompt

"Write an essay on the concept of foreshadowing in African literary works of art. Use a professional tone and voice. Use academic-specific language and terminology, provide detailed and straightforward data, and support your argument with research, expert perspectives, and statistics."

Conversational writing. The essence of this style is to be friendly, informal, relatable, and approachable. To achieve this in your interaction with ChatGPT, your voice, and tone have to be like a real-life conversation. You use conversational styles in your blog posts, social media posts, emails, personal statements, and product descriptions.

Sample Prompt

"Write a blog post on the best pizzas in Texas. Your text should be warm, and lighthearted as if you're talking to friends. Make use of conversational tone and voice."

Empathic Writing. Yes, I remember saying that ChatGPT has some level of empathy and I still stand by it. This writing style has to have traces of sensitivity, empathy, compassion, and understanding. For one to connect with an audience on an emotional level and build trust, this style is necessary. You don't see yourself telling your prospective customers something like, *"Buy this clipper or risk looking like an accused criminal who just got out of detention,"* do you? That would be cringy and insensitive. Instead, you could just say, *"Get that fresh haircut that you deserve."* So, when do you appropriate this style? You need it for customer support, health-related contexts, social issues, and personal development.

Sample Prompt

"Write a self-help manual for teenagers on how to handle feelings of low self-esteem. Use a tone and voice that's empathetic."

Simple writing. You only need straightforward, simple, and short sentences in this style. No jargon or complex vocabulary. If your goal is to make information easy to consume for your reader/audience, this is the style to adopt. This style is appropriate for writing a guide or manual, creating marketing resources, writing children's books, writing for individuals with cognitive or language deficiencies, creating content for social media pages or blogs, writing emails, and memos to prospective customers, clients, or colleagues.

Sample Prompt
"Explain ChatGPT in five sentences. Make use of simple language, break down complex parts into simple-to-understand models, and provide hands-on examples and takeaways."

Creative Writing. This is where imaginative, emotional, and vivid language comes to play. You just might end up reading a creative output of your prompt and competing with other poets like you. I couldn't bring myself to mention literary giants like Williams Shakespeare and Christopher Marlowe who wrote masterpieces with their quills and intellects. It would be like committing an unpardonable sin. Those were literary beasts, if you ask me. Do you have ideas and are struggling to put together the right words to put the words together? You've got help. You get to employ literary devices like simile, metaphor, personification, litotes, puns, and so on. Creative writing styles are good for short stories or novels, crafting a poem, a script for TV, writing the perfect social media caption or post, developing content for a class on creative writing, or a personal memoir or essay with a distinctive voice and style.

Sample Prompt

"Write a poem about a girl who gets lost in a desert and finds her way back with the help of a stranger. Use vivid language to incite imagery, tone, and atmosphere. Make use of metaphors and personification."

Customizing and Personalizing Your ChatGPT Experience

With all we've discussed so far, it's clear that you can fine-tune your ChatGPT experience to perform specific functions based on your taste or preferences. Besides, you're the boss. ChatGPT won't give you what you want if you don't tell it. Who goes to an eatery and tells the attendant, "I want food?" You have to place an order, which specifically states what you would like to have.

To personalize your recommendations, consider the following practices:

- Make sure your prompt is clear, concise, and specific.

- Consciously and consistently provide feedback to ChatGPT. When you do this, you understand your preferences and give relevant recommendations.

- Explore the content that's recommended. It just might be the content you need or you might even discover something new, intriguing, and interesting.

- Don't hesitate to try out new topics, ideas, or authors. This is a great opportunity to discover new content that you might not have known about or considered.

With an AI model like ChatGPT, you've got yourself a teacher, event planner, dietitian, and so on. It can be whatever you want it to be.

Here's how to tailor your ChatGPT to act according to your needs. Let's use the illustration of the eatery. Let's say you tell an attendant that you want coffee. That's a bit specific. But to get unique, you might say, *"Please, can I have some sugar, cream, and ginger flavor in my coffee?"* Now, your coffee doesn't have to be like the coffee of the next person. That's how customizing your ChatGPT is.

1. Train ChatGPT to Learn Your Writing Style

Interact with ChatGPT regularly and provide feedback to train it to understand your unique writing style. This will help you receive more accurate and personalized responses.

Example Prompt: *"Analyze the text below and write a new paragraph using (state your writing style) on the topic - (type out the topic too)."*

2. Brainstorm for Fresh Ideas

When you're running out of ideas for social media posts, blogs, or newsletters, use ChatGPT to brainstorm new and exciting content ideas that will engage your audience.

Example Prompt: *"Provide ten creative ideas for [your objective]"*

3. Specify Content for More Detailed Responses

For more in-depth responses, be specific about the type of content you want from ChatGPT. Whether it's a detailed guideline, an informative article, or a step-by-step process, you can tailor the responses to suit your needs.

Example Prompt: *"Create a comprehensive guide on [Topic], including subheadings and bullet points, with a friendly and informative tone. The target readers are [Users]."*

4. Summarize for a Better Understanding

When faced with lengthy or complex answers, ask ChatGPT to summarize the essential details to make them easier to understand and digest.

Example Prompt: *"Summarize this article on [Topic] in five key points."*

5. Change Writing Style for Better Readability

If you have articles that need to be more engaging or accessible, ChatGPT can help by changing the writing style to match your desired tone or voice.

Example Prompt: *"Rewrite the following text to be more humorous and engaging."*

3

INTELLIGENT PROMPTING TECHNIQUES

No matter how sophisticated or powerful our thinking machines become, there still will be two kinds of people: those who let the machines do their thinking for them, and those who tell the machines what to think about.

— C. J. LEWIS

Have you ever watched an amateur actor on TV? If you're anything like me, you must have asked yourself, *"What the heck is this person doing on TV? Don't they have someone in charge of casting or something?"* You notice that a particular actor seems out of place, struggling with a particular role. There are likely to be two problems here — that the person is not that much of an actor and finds it difficult to interpret the role, or the director/producer is doing a pretty messed up job by not giving certain instructions to bring out the best from the actor.

When it comes to ChatGPT, you can't afford to leave everything to chance. ChatGPT is what you make it to be. It's a good role-player if you offer it the right prompts. The destiny of the output is all in your hands.

How can you ask intelligent and high-quality input prompts? I know we've spoken briefly about prompts in the previous chapter. But that's just scratching the surface. You already know about jailbreaking — the process of tricking ChatGPT into giving you certain answers it hasn't been programmed to give. There's more. There are outputs, but there are high-quality outputs that you can get. Prompts are meant to ensure clarity, focus, and relevance in your project. After reading this, you'll thank me and realize that you might have been doing some things wrong in your conversations with ChatGPT.

This is the part where you roll up your sleeves. Getting the best out of this model requires guiding the model's output to ensure its relevance. This is where prompt engineering comes in.

I didn't mention this earlier but you need to know that there's a prompt formula. They have three elements:

- **Role:** The model has to take on a role to carry out a task. It could be the role of a marketer, inventor, therapist, copywriter, journalist, advertiser, and so on.

- **Task:** A clear and crisp input stating exactly what the prompt wants the model to achieve according to the role that you've assigned to it.

- **Instructions:** You don't just enter an input. Back it up with instructions.

The essence of learning prompting techniques is based on the fact that ChatGPT may not always produce the preferred output if proper guidance is absent. Let's get to it, shall we?

Crafting Effective Prompts

Before I continue, I need to trash this mindset that might have been leaving you to toss and turn in bed at night. Don't see ChatGPT as an AI that's threatening to take over your job. See it as a model that's replacing the most tedious aspects of your job. Be mindful not to use it to replace a task that you could easily have handled yourself. Ease can be addictive, closely followed by over-reliance. Trust me.

Let's get back to business. The following are the different methods for crafting effective prompts:

1. The Instructions Prompt Technique

Here you provide specific instructions so your output is just what you had imagined. For example, if you want to write a blog post for your company, you'll provide a task such as, "Write a blog post about the best sneakers for athletes for a business that sells sneakers."

Your instruction should then be, *"Responses should be warm, friendly, and conversational."*

Prompt Formula: Write a blog post about sneakers for athletes, following these instructions: The responses should be warm, friendly, and conversational.

2. Role Prompting Technique

This technique is all about deciding the output of ChatGPT by giving a specific role that you want the model to take on. The role prompting technique is just perfect if you're targeting a particular type of audience or want it tailored to a particular context.

So how do you do this? Make clear the role you want the model to take on. If you're trying to generate a copy for a gas gauge, you would need to provide a role like copywriting.

Therefore, your prompt formula would be: *"Generate a short-form copy for a gas gauge company as a copywriter."*

3. Information-seeking Prompts

These prompts are designed to help you find specific information. They typically answer questions starting with "What" and "How." For example, you might ask, "What are the health benefits of green tea?" or "How do I change the oil in my car?"

4. Chained Prompts

Since there are limits to the length of response that ChatGPT gives, you need to write your prompt in a way that is tailored according to your needs. How do you achieve this? By adding specific information and keywords so it's all-encompassing.

For example,

Task: You want to write a blog post on the best moving company in California for a website.

If you feel it's going to be a post that you want to be comprehensive, you can ask ChatGPT to write a blog post for a health website.

Prompt: *"Write a blog post of not less than 30 words of web page content about – The best moving company in California. Then include 3 bullet points that must include keywords like best movers, moving company, and transportation.*

The above is very specific.

5. Seed Word Prompt

In this case, you control the output by entering a seed word or phrase, followed by an instruction, "Generate an article based on the following seed word."

For example,

Task: Generate an article about Mount Everest

Seed words: Mount Everest, Expedition

Prompt formula: *"Generate text based on the seed words: Mount Everest, Expedition.*

ChatGPT would proceed to spout out an interesting article related to an expedition by skilled climbers scaling Mount Everest, detailing their journey of self-discovery and camaraderie.

6. Scamper Method

This is a creative way that involves strategies such as substitute, combine, adapt, modify, repurpose, reverse, and eliminate.

Original prompt: Write an essay about the invention of the automobile

Substitute: *"Write an essay about the history of robots."*

Combine: *"Write an essay about the history of robots and their impact on humanity."*

Adapt: *"Write an essay about the history of robots and why it has come to stay."*

Modify: *"Write an essay about the evolution of robots over the past two decades."*

Put to another use: *"Write a short story about robots that were enslaved in a nation, only to rebel after 10 years of labor."*

Eliminate: *"Write a story about a robot."*

Reverse: *"Write a short story about robots that were slaves for a nation, only to realize that one of them was human."*

There are many other techniques that we can't fully exhaust here. But knowing this will be a stepping stone to discovering more prompting techniques.

Utilizing Contextual Information in Your Prompts

Have you ever been in a situation when you took offense over something someone said to you via text because you didn't understand the context of the statement? It's one of the reasons why I prefer one-on-one conversations or phone calls. If it's a one-on-one conversation, context is easy. You're able to see where the person is coming from, through tone of voice and body language.

But texts can make understanding texts quite tricky, so more effort needs to be put into making things clearer. Thankfully, emojis are there to make light of a statement that might have a wrong effect if left in isolation.

When it comes to communication, remember that what a person says is not always what he or she means.

How can you utilize contextual information in your prompts? First, you need to understand what contextual information suggests.

This has to do with certain information that's not ambiguous and is meant for a certain meaning and purpose, even though it could have other meanings and intents. It has to do with the background knowledge which provides a pathway to a deeper understanding of an event, person, or detail.

As is the case with many industries, contextual information is used to boost the evaluation of collected data to make it more efficient in deciphering behavior patterns or improving customer experience.

How can you utilize contextual information in your prompts?

1. **Consider the task definition.** Lay out the purpose of the task and instructions that the model needs to carry out. For example, you don't just write, *"Write a CV."* You need to add more information like the career you're pursuing, your experi-

ences, and other pieces of information that you think will be helpful. Instead, your prompt can be,

> *"Write a CV for someone who has a degree in Accountancy from Ohio State University. Use the following details to construct the resume:*
> *Objective*
> *Work experience*
> *Professional Experience*
> *Awards*
> *Published works*
> *References*

It will get you the desired output if you provide context to every prompt that you put in.

2. **Your prompt has to convey the intent of the user** so that AI will have an idea of the information that you're looking out for. Since you have a task at hand the intent has to be included.

For example, you could structure your prompt into something like, *"Write a cover letter of someone who has a degree in Accountancy and wants to apply for a job in an oil company."*

The user's intent is clear in the prompt. A prompt that doesn't have a user intent can look like, *"Write a cover letter for someone who has a degree in Accountancy."* That's vague and lacks proper context.

3. **Narrow down your topics.** Your output will lack depth if you don't narrow down topics that you know are quite broad. If you're looking for something specific, you need to write a narrowed-down prompt.

For example, *"Write an essay on imposter syndrome."* It's vague, right? But if you want something in-depth, you can instead write, *"Write an essay on imposter syndrome among female African-American students in college."*

4. Frame the responses through specific instructions. To provide the right context, set up expectations with your prompts. How do you want it? Formal or informal? Conversational or professional? What role do you want the model to play that will determine the preciseness of your output? Framing begins with adding the style that you prefer to your instruction.

For example, *"Write a blog post on staying warm in winter. The blog should be instructional and conversational."*

You have yourself a role player and a game changer when you understand that contextualized language is how to get the best output from ChatGPT.

Utilizing ChatGPT's Natural Language

You already know that human-like conversations are possible with ChatGPT. This language model is known to answer your questions and follow up on conversations. Without doubt, ChatGPT harnesses a multitude of advanced technologies to achieve fast and precise outputs. The natural language processing (NLP) component especially plays a pivotal role in enabling natural-sounding conversations. NLP strategies like tokenization break sentences into tiny pieces for easier processing. Entity recognition identifies important information like names and places. Sentiment analysis identifies and understands emotions in text, while part-of-speech tagging helps identify grammatical word roles like nouns, verbs and adjectives. Therefore, if you can skillfully fine-tune your prompts, ChatGPT can discern sentiment and purpose in your prompt language to provide the appropriate outputs.

With NLP, ChatGPT can complete tasks like writing codes, translating, debugging, searching for recipes, and writing articles and blogs.

Examples of natural language processing include:

1. Email filters
2. Customer-service automation
3. Machine translation
4. Social media monitoring
5. Text Analytics
6. Predictive Text
7. Assistant
8. Fraud Detection
9. Text Analytics
10. Summarization Application

How are you as an individual taking advantage of NLP? You might have begun unknowingly. In case you don't know, here they are:

- With deep learning, ChatGPT interprets queries and allows them to converse accurately.

- You get to build conversational AI applications, fast and easily without prior training or effort.

- Interactions are more personalized for every user by using dynamic memory networks, which can follow up on conversations across different platforms and devices.

Optimizing Prompt Length and Structure for Improved Outcomes

You want to get the best out of ChatGPT, but there's the issue of prompt limit. The prompt limit is the maximum number of words that you can enter into the text box. Here are tips to find your way around it:

1. Keep it short, simple, and straightforward. If the input is long, an error message will pop up. Even spaces between texts are equivalent to a word.

2. While it's short and simple, make sure that context is provided. Do this by writing a short background on a certain topic, and backing it up with necessary keywords.

3. If there's so much knowledge shared in a chat, it's best to start a new chat so that the context of the conversation is maintained.

4. Pay attention to the length of your prompt. The limits vary, but generally, it accepts 2048 characters, including spaces.

5. Pay attention to context also.

6. If you're focused on improving content generation, focus on keywords, major characters, and stories.

Using Feedback Loops

Feedback loops play a crucial role in the success of any AI system (Robinson, 2023). It allows continuous improvement of the model by evaluating its performance and making necessary adjustments. The loop involves taking the machine learning algorithm's output, comparing it with actual results, and using this information to fine-tune the algorithm's parameters.

ChatGPT is a really cool tool, but sometimes it can get things wrong or give weak answers. Understanding the feedback loop can help us improve and avoid these issues with AI models. It's like learning from mistakes to get better and smarter responses.

Let's say you want to plan a dream vacation. You can start by asking ChatGPT for destination ideas. Once you have a list of potential places, prompt the AI to think of 10 exciting activities you can do in each location. After that, ask the AI to consider any potential challenges or drawbacks for each activity and come up with 10 ways to overcome them.

Continue the loop by asking ChatGPT, "You sure?" This process helps refine and optimize your vacation plans based on the AI's own evaluations and suggestions.

By engaging in this feedback loop, you'll have a well-rounded and improved travel itinerary that covers the best destinations, exciting activities, and smart solutions to potential obstacles. This approach ensures you get the most accurate and reliable recommendations.

Ethical Considerations of ChatGPT

1. **AI tools can have access to your data.** Be sure of what you're giving up. Time and time again, we've learned that when we use any online tool, we expose or give up some of our data, and AI tools aren't any different.

2. **The tool might replace your work if you don't restrict it to improving it.** It should make it easier and better not to do all of your work. It's okay to write an essay yourself, while you ask ChatGPT to correct your grammatical errors. A student can ask ChatGPT for tips on how to make a copy more attention-grabbing. However, don't trust the bot too blindly. Pay attention to your intuition. Note also that if you produce a piece of work using the tool, give credit to the bot and other authors.

3. **Information obtained from ChatGPT isn't immune to bias.**

Be careful not to accept every piece of information obtained from the ChatGPT. It could propagate harmful stereotypes. Imagine ChatGPT being the source of social media content. Think of the havoc it would cause, from spreading fake news to the dangerous uproar it might incite over sensitive topics.

4. **Since GPT-3 is trained on a lot of data, the data sources are sometimes questionable.** Who puts stuff on the internet? You bet it wasn't Zeus and Merlin. Humans like us upload information to the internet, and it's human to make mistakes.

5. **ChatGPT can encourage cheating.** I'm afraid there might be a drop in enthusiasm to learn in no time. What will education be like in the next two years? Is education soon to become ordinarily a part of a checklist shoved on us by our parents or a passion and avenue to see and understand the world?

6. **ChatGPT lacks moral judgment and empathy.** Have you found yourself asking ChatGPT questions you wouldn't dare ask your friends? You're likely to see responses without emotional context or empathy pop up. If you want some cuddles, you know who to call. But it's definitely not AI.

ChatGPT is one of the greatest innovations in the world in these tech times. But it needs to be put on a leash.

PART II

—

MONETIZING CHATGPT WITH EASE

I wanted to start this part with a joke about money, but then I was out. And I didn't want to risk telling a joke that wasn't funny. Guess what I did? Yep. I asked ChatGPT. It gave me twelve jokes instantly. I'll let you in on my favorite two.

1. *"What's a rich person's favorite song? 'Can't Buy Me Love' by The Beatles!"*
2. *"Why did the banker switch careers? He lost interest!"*

Blimey! Cool stuff.

Then ChatGPT told me: These are only playful jokes. Money's importance goes way beyond jokes. I rolled my eyes. Like I didn't know.

Monetizing ChatGPT sounds a little bleh. Let's see how to make super cool bucks with ChatGPT. Yeah, that's better. Let's go.

4

MAXIMIZING EARNING POTENTIAL

"Once a new technology rolls over you, if you're not part of the steamroller, you're part of the road."

— STEWART BRAND

Have you heard about Jackson Greathouse Fall? Well, this is a man who asked ChatGPT to grant him instructions on how to convert $100 into a lot of money. He paid heed to the instructions of the chatbot, and in a few days, he had created more than $1,378 worth of affiliate marketing websites. Another user has claimed to have made $6,147 in a week.

Do you get the point now?

You can make money from ChatGPT.

The potential of ChatGPT isn't just in its efficiency and productivity. It's a treasure chest you can unlock if you know your onions. This model is making more money from freelancers and even leading to the rise of more entrepreneurs. Now that the gig economy keeps rising at a fast pace, we have more people offering virtual assistant services with the help of ChatGPT. For different business functions, money-smart individuals are selling the idea of a customized chatbot to various businesses. In no time, prompt building will become a major career for some people. Freelancers can boldly raise their shoulders high because of how much work has been made easy through this AI technology. They can no longer see themselves losing clients to a lack of efficiency.

Exploring Freelancing Opportunities

An interviewer once asked the CEO of Upwork if the rise of ChatGPT meant the death of freelancing. This doomsday talk is not uncommon when something new is introduced to the public. According to the CEO, ChatGPT and freelancers are more allies than competitors. Hmm. How accurate. Clients are still outsourcing to freelancers, with some stating that knowledge of ChatGPT is a requirement. So, don't think that you're on the back burner if you're a freelancer or if you're considering freelancing. In fact, you're not at all at risk because the irony of it all is that although ChatGPT can do all these amazing things and write stories and all that, its invention has rather heightened the sensitivity of many people to AI content. And there's never been a time when originality was more valued. So, chill. Make this ChatGPT your ally, your assistant, and you're going to shine like the sun.

Back to the topic of freelancing opportunities. When it comes to ChatGPT and freelancing, the keyword you're looking for is automation. This stuff right here is what separates the boys from the men when it comes to discussions about productivity. Automation helps you create a system that can make your entire freelancing journey a breeze—easier than harder, and yes, with better productivity, you're very likely to earn more.

While freelancing is a very wide sector, the main processes are largely similar: get hired, do the job, and deliver, right? But that's not even where I'm going. The processes that produce an amazing result for any freelancer are highlighted by excellent research. That research process is one way that you can leverage ChatGPT so much that you'll be surprised.

Do you know that if you're in academia, you can leverage your research experience to make money for yourself?

Did you know that you can secure a contract as a research consultant? You can leverage your research skills and expertise by providing consulting services to individuals, organizations, and businesses. You get to assist in designing research methodologies, analyzing data, providing valuable insights, and interpreting the results of your research. Using ChatGPT, you get to handle all of this without sweating. Research consulting cuts across different fields, such as the health sector, social sciences, engineering, and so on.

Science and technical writing require a lot of research. Researching requires that you explain and communicate complex concepts through your blog posts, articles, science-related websites, or magazines. Gradually, you become an authority in this field and optimize your income in the long run. ChatGPT is capable of handling technical terms and helping you break them down for the average reader to understand.

Now that online learning is becoming more popular and in high demand, there's a frantic search for subject matter experts. Through research, you can create and develop online courses and offer expert guidance in your chosen field of expertise. This way, you're able to share your wealth of knowledge with the growth of others. Your work gets easier because you're already a master in your field and are capable of engineering your prompts to bring out the desired outputs for your research.

Data Analysis and visualization are important skills in the

industry. And research sometimes requires statistical analysis and programming. With the help of data visualization tools, you can provide services to businesses, startups, and research organizations. Your expertise will help clients make data-driven decisions, and identify trends. After you're done with your evaluation, you can present your findings to your clients in a visually appealing way.

Can you see the opportunities that abound with ChatGPT? While you think this is a side hustle for you, you'll realize that it has become a major aspect of your career that's bringing in more bucks than what you see as your main job.

The nature of work and careers is changing. If you want to maximize opportunities, this is the time to hit the ground running.

Here's a highlight of the freelancing opportunities that you can explore with ChatGPT:

1. Freelance writing and editing
2. Blogging and affiliate marketing
3. Content Creation for Social Media
4. Self-publishing of e-books
5. Online courses and coaching
6. Email marketing and newsletters
7. Language translation services
8. Virtual assistance
9. Resume and cover letter writing
10. Copywriting and advertising
11. Market research and data analysis
12. SEO optimization
13. Creative writing services
14. Ghostwriting
15. Speechwriting
16. Scriptwriting

17. Social media management
18. Customer support
19. Technical writing
20. AI-generated art
21. E-commerce Product Descriptions
22. Crowd-funding campaign content
23. Personalized AI-generated content
24. Custom AI chatbot development

Leveraging ChatGPT for Content Creation and Copywriting

Have you ever watched some video content and said to yourself, "Wow! This is a great promotional video." You'd gotten so carried away by the entertaining nature of the video that you didn't know where it was headed until you realized that it was just an ad. But you had fun watching it, didn't you?

That's how magical content creation can be. But it can be more when you leverage AI. As for copywriting, you know how long it takes to come up with catchy headlines exclusive to a project. Well, good news! You no longer have to spend hours brainstorming when you can brainstorm on an AI model like ChatGPT. Note that content creation involves both written content and video content. But first, let's take a good look at ChatGPT and content creation.

Content creation is an avenue for digital marketers, SEO specialists, and content marketers to let people into what they have to offer, whether it's a product or service. If you're going to delve into email marketing, you also need to create content. How can you, as a marketer, use ChatGPT?

A recent LinkedIn survey by Smart Insights showed that more than three-quarters of marketers desire to use ChatGPT to boost their marketing performance. However, just 40% are living up to that desire (Chaffey, 2023).

I understand that it's difficult to know where to start, but you've got to start anyway. As a content marketer, what prompts should you explore to get the best content ideas?

ChatGPT can help you generate ideas for content in areas like engaging Q&A, PR and media outreach, information sources, promotions, calls-to-action, and images.

You need to master the art of generating prompts for anything that's content-related.

Concerning engaging Q&A ideas for content, you can ask the model, *"What are some frequently asked questions about [topic] that can be used to create engaging and fun content."* If it's for a video, you can always indicate it.

If you're seeking an idea that's newsworthy for PR or media outreach, ChatGPT can help you create stories worth telling, attention-grabbing stories. There are so many creative and interesting ideas that ChatGPT will keep you hooked. You can use prompts like, *"Generate newsworthy topics or events related to [company or industry] that can be useful for PR and media outreach."* If you're using ChatGPT-4, you can go a step further by asking the model to *"Browse the web to provide current newsworthy subjects connected to the [company /industry] for events and media outreach."*

Email Marketing ideas and strategies will be a walk in the park with the help of ChatGPT. Email marketing is a strategic way to reach and nurture potential customers. You can ask the model to *"Generate effective email marketing strategies to engage subscribers and drive conversion."* With ChatGPT Plus, you go a step further by asking the model to review your website to come up with an idea.

For promotions and sales-focused content, you're covered. You can get creative with promotions to encourage customers to take action. Using prompts like this, you can ignite strong persuasion through your content. *"Generate ideas for fun-filled and engaging promotions and sales content to drive customers to take a purchasing action."*

To make people aware of your brand, social media is the place to be. With ChatGPT, you can brainstorm ideas for campaigns, posts, and activities that will increase your followership online. You can ask the model to *"Briefly generate 5 ideas for social media captions that can attract followers."*

If you are looking for images and media to bring your content to life, you can use ChatGPT to get suggestions on what can make your content more visually appealing. Since the average person on social media has a short attention span, especially when reading texts, images are a good way to keep things fresh and lively. Your prompt can be like this, *"Suggest images and media that are suitable to enhance and complement my post on [topic]."*

Copywriting just got more interesting. How many times have you brainstormed on the perfect copy and still didn't come up with anything for days?

Copywriting still falls under content creation, and it goes beyond writing ads and promo copies. Other aspects of copywriting would need the help of ChatGPT. As a copywriter, you need help creating documents and outlines that will give you the pieces of information that you need to get the job done. You'll need to do some target audience research or look for ways to describe a product better. You need all the help that you can get. I won't bore you with the many other things that copywriters do. But there are copywriting prompts that reflect the many functions of a copywriter. Let's get down to business.

Prompt for customer persona and target market. For example, *"I am selling [a product] with the following product description: [enter a detailed description of the product]. Who is likely going to indicate interest in this product? Who's my target audience? Generate a customer persona for this product."*

Prompt for landing page copy. For example, *"With the information below about my product and my customer persona, suggest 250 words for a landing page selling [enter product] to new prospective customers. The copy should be persuasive to convince prospects to patronize my business."*

Email Marketing. For example, *Write a persuasive email body copy for my [enter product/keyword] with a subject line of [enter the subject line]. The detailed description of [insert product description or keyword] is [insert product description].*

Product Page Copy. *"Create a compelling product page, including a short description of my product, a long detailed description of my product, and five bullet points to persuade and convince people to make a buying decision."*

Press Release Copy. For example, *"Kindly help me write a press release telling people about [insert product/keyword] and sell them why that production is a need for them. Write in an active voice, don't plagiarize, and speak directly to the customer based on my customer persona."*

Google Ads Ad Copy. For example, *"Generate 20 Google Ads headlines with 30 characters. The headline should persuade people to buy my [enter product/keyword] and it should sell customers on the benefits of [enter the product or keyword].*

Other things that you can do are generate social media prompts, generate emotion-based copies, ask ChatGPT to suggest taglines or hooks for your products, create Google ad descriptions, and so on. You can write great ads with this model. Ensure that your prompts are compelling and aren't generic if you want to elicit the best responses out of ChatGPT that are meaningful, satisfying and thought-provoking.

Other ways that you can go about your content with ChatGPT are:

- Improving your content.

- Crafting winning emails
- Writing captivating social media captions
- Writing product descriptions
- Making content more readable
- Finding keywords and high-ranking keywords
- Personalizing your content
- Managing SEO analytics

Enhancing Customer Support and Chatbot Services

Gone are the days when customers queued in front of an officer who was all cranky and feeling disorganized because of overwhelming complaints. ChatGPT helps you build chatbots well-tailored for your business model, so you can easily attend to customers without stress. As a business, you can create chatbots that help with HR tasks, employee onboarding, and scheduling.

In addition, your chatbot can facilitate sales and marketing, let prospective customers know about the details of your products and services, and assist you in generating leads. When it comes to business processes, chatbots simplify them. The responses that the chatbot helps to generate are human-like and capable of understanding context and assisting in various tasks.

I'll give you tips to optimize your Customer service using chatbots.

1. Leverage Stored Data for Better Communication

Make sure your chatbot can access stored data about customers' preferences and personal information. This way, it can engage with users more effectively and quickly address their needs and concerns.

2. Adding a Human Touch to Your Brand with Chatbots

Add human-like elements to your chatbot interactions to make customers feel understood and valued. Mimicking human interaction and using stored data to identify pain points will help build brand loyalty and convert visitors into customers.

3. Provide Stellar and Speedy Support

Customers expect fast solutions to their problems. Use chatbots to offer real-time, round-the-clock support that moves customers through the sales funnel. This ensures a smooth user experience and strengthens customer loyalty.

4. Personalize Recommendations with Chatbots

Train your chatbot to provide personalized product recommendations based on user preferences and browsing history. This tailored approach enhances the user experience and helps customers find relevant products more easily.

Automating Data Analysis and Decision-Making Processes

It's no news that one of the strengths of AI is being able to interpret large amounts of data. This process includes looking out for patterns and adding them into reports, documents, and clear formats. It's what data analysts and other knowledge economy professionals have to deal with regularly.

In the decision-making of any company, data analysis can't be ignored. Data Analysis requires computer processes and systems to perform analytical tasks without human intervention.

It has been in existence for many years. Since the 1960s, it has been an instrument of operational support in industrial systems. The academic world hasn't hesitated to reflect on how data analysis keeps evolving and what it signifies to the end user. In generic terms, there are four major categories. We have: descriptive, diagnostic, predictive, and prescriptive.

Descriptive analysis examines data manually to find answers to the questions, "What happened?" or "What's happening?" and is characterized by traditional business brainpower and illustrations like pie charts, line graphs, tables, bar charts, or generated narratives.

Diagnostic analysis is a more innovative form of data analysis. It analyzes data to discover answers to questions like "Why did it happen?" and has strategies including data discovery, data mining, drill down, and correlations. The human intervention in this type of analysis is high.

Predictive analysis is more advanced than the previous categories because it's about knowing what's coming. It seeks to answer the question, "What is going to happen?" or "What's happening next?" The strategies connected to this type of analysis are forecasting, pattern matching, predictive modeling, regression, and multivariate statistics. Artificial Intelligence plays a significant role in more innovative data analysis.

A prescriptive analysis is the most advanced of all the categories. It utilizes data to augment decision-making. It answers, "What must be done?" or "What can be done to make it happen?"

What's the connection between data analysis of decision-making? Relax, I'll break everything down. Businesses use this data from the analysis to understand better: transcending observation to gain valuable insights, and beyond insight, into the domain of forecasting and predicting trends that is yet to come.

Your business needs to be able to extract a meaningful understanding of products or services, the processes involved, the production, the gains, maintenance, and manufacturing functions, make decisions, and take proactive steps when necessary. Dear reader, this will determine the growth and profitability of your business. Let me blow your mind a little further. Here are the areas data analysis will play out in your business:

- Improving the quality of products and services
- Improving customer support

- Increasing production through input
- Improving yield/earnings
- Predicting and/or preventing maintenance
- Speeding up takeoff time
- Improving supply chain operations.

What advantage does ChatGPT have over traditional analysis?

1. ChatGPT not only helps you analyze your data, but generates reports on details about your customer — sentiment and behavior, to improve the customer experience. You get to analyze the financial state of your business, spot trends, make more decisions from a place of insight, and improve financial performance. Input a dataset related to a particular subject or person and wait for the analysis output.

2. It helps analyze disorganized data like customer reviews, social media posts, or captions to reveal valuable insights to determine any intended business decision.

3. It assists you in getting insights and recommendations. As a data analyst, you need insight. These insights will then lead to the model making recommendations based on the output of the dataset you put in it.

4. Your process gets automated. Instead of waiting for reports to get generated, your data is processed at top speed so you can make decisions in real time. Whenever there's a market change, your business or client responds swiftly to it, which means staying ahead of the competition.

5. Helps discover how charts, graphs, and other infographics and data visualizations could be constructed, and what other information needs to be included.

6. ChatGPT can also help figure out where to identify data sources that have the probability of providing the insights

needed for a particular task. For example, "Where can I find data on cyber fraud in developing countries?"

7. You can generate synthetic data for various purposes, like training other machine learning models or testing algorithms.

8. ChatGPT helps define data structures, like what fields need to be part of a database or what row and column headings for a spreadsheet.

Optimizing SEO and Content Marketing Strategies

While every business owner wants to rank high on Google, you can't rank high just by wishing for it or swinging a magical wand. There are tools that you need to have at your disposal. Search engine optimization (SEO) is the way you can optimize your content for search engines. The good thing is that ChatGPT can optimize your content for search engines. How?

- **It can generate blog post ideas for your website.**
  For example,

  Prompt: *"Generate blog ideas for a moving company."*
  Prompt: *"Generate content marketing ideas for a skincare business."*

- **It can generate relevant keywords for your articles and blog posts.** For example,

  Prompt: *"Generate keywords for content marketing for a cake business."*
  Prompt: *"Generate LSI keywords for content marketing."*

- **Create an organized structure for your blog and webpage with ChatGPT.** You can enter the following prompt:

Prompt: *"Generate a blog structure for 'Things to consider before studying abroad'."*

- **Generate Attractive SEO titles.** There are many SEO titles that ChatGPT can help you generate, which can attract leads. Here's an example:

Prompt: *"Craft creative SEO titles for the topic: harnessing the benefits of Vitamin D."*

But I want you to know that Google has algorithms that recognize AI-generated content. So I'd strongly advise that you adjust your content to make it more raw and relevant.

- **You can generate meta description tags that are highly converting with content that will keep your audience glued.**

Prompt: *"Generate a meta description for 'Benefits of content marketing' in 150 characters."*

- **Create a high-quality FAQ tailored for your website.**

Prompt: *"Generate a FAQ for my online course, 'Digital Marketing and your business'."*

Since you need to research the market you're going into,

ChatGPT will help you at the initial stage, where you're still brainstorming ideas. With the help of the tool, you can develop fresh ideas and concepts to explore, you can develop novel research topics, tailor your hypotheses, or develop marketing campaigns that might not have been considered in the first place.

When it comes to your marketing plans and product development, you can get valuable knowledge concerning consumer behavior and preferences. You'll even get suggestions on innovative variables that you can include in the study and also suggest future approaches.

You don't need to spend so much money on hiring a team of human analysts. Thankfully, free or cheap NLP APIs are useful for that aspect of work.

You'll get insights for your marketing campaigns, and customer service decisions, as you can use ChatGPT to assess real-time data.

You might be wondering about the prospects of marketing with ChatGPT in the building. Rivas and Zhao (2023) asserted that ChatGPT has the ability to optimize all marketing activities, including consumers' behavior, if provided with the right amount of data.

When it comes to consumer behavior, ChatGPT will help you understand why customers act in a certain way, like choosing to patronize a brand over another.

Even as a consumer, ChatGPT will help you in the area of information processing. For example, if you want to buy a tablet, ChatGPT can suggest, recommend, and compare tablets, breaking down the technical specifications and product features for you.

If you want to make good money from marketing, keep in mind that your target audience is your only concern. You want to impress them. You want them to trust you. You want them to see you as an authority. You want them to buy from you. This is where branding comes in.

ChatGPT's got your back when it comes to analyzing social media and other online data. This is to know how your prospective customers perceive a brand or product. You also have the privilege of knowing areas of strength and weakness concerning brand perception. From here, you make moves to improve customer loyalty and reputation.

Sales are no big deal for ChatGPT. The model can help you predict sales and future income through an analysis of past market trends, data, and customer behavior.

ChatGPT as a Virtual Assistant

As a small business owner, hiring a virtual assistant might have crossed your mind. You need help with small tasks like answering emails, writing content for your website, attending to customers, and so on. The problem here is that you're doing all of these by yourself. Pfft! I know how draining it can be. It gets even more exhausting when the thought of undone tasks crosses your mind. Here are ways you can use ChatGPT as that virtual assistant to take care of your little but important tasks and help you make money in your online business:

1. You get help with emails, like writing pitches to potential clients and proposals to leads you're already engaging. I know there are times you get blank about how to construct your thoughts, sound as persuasive as possible, and keep the engagement warm. All you need to do is send a prompt like, *"Write me a persuasive email pitch to a potential client on why you're the perfect web content writer for their business."* You can include more details about your products or services, using instructions that will make the email brief but friendly.

2. Do you need help with content marketing? You've got

yourself an assistant. We all know that content marketing is time-consuming, ranging from coming up with ideas related to your industry to constructing your thoughts into words. Be more specific with your requests within each of the general ideas that ChatGPT has provided for you. You can begin by asking it to create an outline for an article about the topic. Afterwards, you can feed ChatGPT with that outline and ask it to write an introduction for a blog article about a subject with a particular topic, following that outline. Here is how you can take advantage of all the potential that ChatGPT has when it comes to content creation and get the best results.

3. ChatGPT helps with your email marketing ideas based on your niche. You're able to sell more products and services to a larger audience. If you feel like you don't know much about email marketing, you can ask ChatGPT to teach you the types of email marketing that are the most popular. Within those types of emails, ChatGPT can help you with ideas that you can integrate into the kind of emails that you plan to write and forward to your email subscribers. Use ChatGPT to follow up on conversations to your advantage. You can add instructions like, *"Make it a bit longer,"* or *"Add more conversational language or humor."*

4. If your website has remained unused for a long time, now is the time to revive it with content or ad copies. Tell ChatGPT about your business model. For your homepage, ask ChatGPT to *"Write a Home Page for my website"* or *"Write the About Page for my website."*

5. You can create a chatbot with ChatGPT. You can have a chat interface on your website integrated with OpenAI's API code, which has you talking to the server more discreetly and training it on what it is that you want it to know, like how to attend to customers and your scheduling process, and integrate it with your scheduling software or calendar. Here is how to create an app that can engage your customers, attend to

complaints, and give you all the necessary information about the needs of both your customers and prospective clients.

6. ChatGPT can assist you in carrying out a client's project. Whatever ChatGPT can do for you, it can do for your client. As an email marketing agency, ChatGPT is there to help you write emails. If it's a branding agency that you're running, this AI model will assist in writing content for your client's business website or coming up with catchy slogans or names for their businesses. And if it's a virtual assistance agency, it can assist with everything from content creation.

7. ChatGPT can play any role, maybe as a coach, teacher, or mentor. You know better by now that ChatGPT doesn't know everything. But it does know so much.

Applying ChatGPT in the E-commerce and Sales Industry

Whether you're into affiliate marketing, dropshipping, or selling your product, ChatGPT can help you step up your marketing game.

Begin by asking ChatGPT about the product you plan to sell and what the best marketing plan is for that product. ChatGPT will suggest suitable social media platforms you can market on to target specific demographics. Another approach is influencer marketing. You can ask for a list of social media influencers in your niche and consider partnering with some of them to promote your product to their followers. Of course, you will be expected to pay a percentage or commission on sales. Additionally, ChatGPT can help with email marketing and SEO optimization, which you may explore after you have gained more experience as a beginner.

You can start with, *"Tell me more about social media marketing"* or *"Tell me more about Influencer marketing."* It will go through its database and provide relevant information about it.

It gets even better. ChatGPT knows how to break down pieces of information for you as if you're a fifth-grader with the prompt *"Explain this to me like I'm a fifth-grader."*

You can perfect your strategy using AI. Find out the marketing strategy that works best for your product. Once you're through, you move on to carrying out more specific tasks.

Let's say that you've already chosen a marketing strategy that you've kick-started. You're running paid ads, taking up influencer marketing, or listing some of your products on Amazon. It's called Amazon FBA (It's sort of similar to dropshipping, but you need to purchase a certain amount of products upfront and have an inventory, and Amazon will store the products for you, ship them to your customers and even attend to the customer service.)

To stand out and make more sales, you must maximize your options. Begin with the product description, title, and other things, including search engine optimization.

Begin by asking ChatGPT to write a description of a product that you intend to sell. You can do this based on what you require from the chatbot or ask it to adjust or improve your content.

If your product already has a description or title, you can copy and paste it on ChatGPT, asking it to improve it.

If you want to sell on a personal e-commerce store

For sellers that aren't selling on any existing marketplace like Amazon.com or eBay and are only doing that on the e-commerce store that you set up through Shopify, ChatGPT can design your webpage, ensuring that it makes a lot of money for you.

That's not all. It can also create an attractive design. For example, if you're selling caps, you can ask ChatGPT to provide six different ideas for a webpage that will be perfect for your eCommerce store. You can look out for a competitor within your niche, take a screenshot of their webpage, and with AI, you can create a similar one and make it even better. How do you go about this strategy? No qualms.

Go to midjourney.com (Mid-journey.com is an AI-based text-to-image software, which converts your requirements into high-quality images.) OpenAI has its version too. It's called DALL-E 2, short for "Dali" and "Wall-E" 2nd iteration. The name is a combination of the surrealist artist Salvador Dalí and the Pixar animated movie character Wall-E. It reflects the AI model's ability to create surreal and artistic images, inspired by the works of Salvador Dalí, and combined with the playful and imaginative character of Wall-E from the movie. Between the two AI generative art software, I'll stick with Midjourney because that's what I prefer.

If you want to sell on Amazon

If you haven't decided on which products to sell, tell ChatGPT to provide you with the winning products sold on Amazon. I'll advise you to focus on non-branded products you can sell on Amazon. Because if you don't state this specifically to ChatGPT, it might provide you with Microsoft products, Macbooks, and even Amazon-branded products that you are not an authorized reseller of.

As a beginner, it's best to stay off branded products because it's hard sourcing them. Also, it won't serve as a strong foundation for your business. Examples of non-branded products that you can sell include foldable storage bins, wireless chargers, face caps, sleeping mats, etc. I didn't think of going into selling these kinds of products until I started using ChatGPT.

I started learning about product research at this point. One product research tool that works well when it comes to selling on Amazon is Helium 10. It's useful when you're faced with so much data and must decide if the product is the right one for sale. Once you install your Google Chrome Extension, there's nothing to worry about. Let's do this step-by-step:

- If you ask ChatGPT for non-branded products you can sell on Amazon, it will give you multiple suggestions. Copy each suggestion and paste them into the Amazon.com search area. After doing this, you'll see a variety of search results.

- Click on the Google Chrome Extension tool and click the icon that reads, "X-ray Amazon product research." A lot of information will pop up, like the number of purchases on an item over the last month and earnings, and the models and designs that customers are buying the most. When it's time to source a product, you would be able to decide which is the best for you to put up for sale to get the best result.

- If you plan on using Helium 10, scroll to the icon "review count" and look out for sellers with the lowest reviews. From here, you know what to expect if you plan on selling the same product.

These are the things to look out for if you plan to sell on Amazon.

If you want to sell on eBay

- Ask ChatGPT to give you the most popular or winning products on eBay. It will give you a list that includes phone cases, jewelry, beauty and skincare products, clothing, craft supplies, pet supplies, etc.

- Let's say you get ChatGPT to tell you the most popular or winning products under craft supplies. It will give you a list of ideas that you can research.

- If you want to research products to sell on eBay, you can try using Zekanalytics.

- Click on product research, change the shipping location to wherever you want, change the eBay site to eBay.com, and click on search. You get information on the amount spent on a product in the past month and the listing rate.

If you want to sell on Shopify

- To build a Shopify store, you must get customers to your website. I'll suggest you use Google Shopping ads. Furthermore, Google Trends is a tool for finding the keywords people are searching for the most.

- ChatGPT comes in when you ask it to give you the most popular non-branded items on Google. Pick a product of your choice and research it. Copy the product that you've chosen, go to Google Trends, and paste it there. Take a good look at the chart that will pop up, giving you information about the search history of the product.

Knowing the winning products on different platforms and your knowledge of product research, you are on your way to building a successful e-commerce business. Note that you need to first sign up for any of these product research software — Helium 10 or Zekanalytics so that you can carry out your product research on your winning products.

Harnessing ChatGPT's Potential for Business Consulting and Strategy

As a business consultant, you're the bearer of ideas and solutions. You help individuals and businesses develop sites, ensure their dream projects come to fruition and that their problems are solved. Here are ways in which you can have ChatGPT assist you as a business consultant and strategist:

Research. Before any decision, some things need to be considered, like researching market data for companies and organizations, background information on market size, etc.

Retrieve Financials and KPI. For example, if you want to look at the revenue data of a company in the past ten years, its profit margins, revenue per employee, KPI (Key Performance Indicator), and so on, traditionally you would have to go through the data that's available yourself. But with ChatGPT, it's easy to retrieve data. For example, you can just ask ChatGPT to give you the profit margin in the movie industry.

Seek out Sources. When you get a request from your project manager to dig out some data, there's the fear of getting data from unreliable sources, which can impede getting relevant data. Therefore, you can ask ChatGPT to provide you with reliable sources to look up market data about the clothing industry in the U.S. It might not give you data, but it might give you reliable sources for your data. It can also provide you with links to access these sources.

Assists in Developing a Hypothesis. At the beginning of a project, brainstorming for ideas begins with knowing company information and looking for information on a subject. Most of the time, there's limited time on your side to formulate ideas for your hypotheses. It might not be 100 percent accurate. So, you can go a step further by asking ChatGPT to get your results double-checked.

Structures the Problems of a Business. In problem-solving, there are three stages: structuring the problem, analyzing it, and communicating the solution. If you can't structure a problem on a powerpoint presentation slide, ChatGPT will help when you ask. For example, you can ask it to structure a particular market. It will provide you with many suggestions. Choose the ones that work for you.

I already taught you how to go about generating prompts. Now you also know in which areas ChatGPT's AI capabilities can be applied. With high-quality prompts and knowing what you want to do, you're on the right track to making the big bucks.

5

BEST PRACTICES FOR EFFICIENCY

"You only have so many hours in a day, let others make the money for you."

— NICK HAAS

At a time when people are bitten by the paranoia bug of fear, some are in awe of AI's ability to save time and improve creativity. One of them is an Indian CEO, Akash Nigam, who was intrigued by the wonders of this innovation.

As a CEO who's hell-bent on making his company more productive and profitable, he bought the premium version of ChatGPT for all his employees. According to him, he had to save hours' of time and even planned to make the use of ChatGPT a part of his employees' performance reviews. Consequently, he spends $2,400 monthly on the premium version of ChatGPT for 120 employees. That's some super intentional energy, if you ask me.

A tweet by a Twitter handle named *Santiago* that read, *"AI will not replace you. A person using AI will."* garnered over 40,000 likes and over 6,000 retweets within a few hours of being tweeted. This isn't far from the truth. The dream of every employer is to have a productive team and get results.

If you've ever been under pressure to beat a deadline, you can relate to the following things: anxiety, feeling disorganized, lack of motivation, shortage of ideas, poor work input, fear of getting fired, pressure to prove yourself, and so on. For many of us, other things are jostling for our attention — kids, our dog, volunteering, religious activities, self-care, family, and so many other important factors in our lives. It can also be frustrating and unfulfilling to have your job as the only thing going on in your life.

Now that ChatGPT is on board, there's little to worry about. Don't you think? Your job and your commitments don't need to suffer.

Managing Time and Prioritizing Tasks with ChatGPT for Productivity

I wouldn't be wrong to say that life gets even busier as we grow older and responsibilities pile up on our shoulders. Time is money, yeah, but it's more than that. Time is a gem, and we want to make sure that some phases of our lives don't suffer at the expense of other aspects of our lives.

As we begin to have a taste of different phases of our lives, we become obligated to learn to schedule our lives and organize our tasks. To be honest, it's not easy. It might seem like twenty-four hours are zooming by so fast, like Mr. Flash from Justice League. But there's a way around things like this. ChatGPT is with its cape, ready to rescue you from your time-related worries and anxiety.

Are there any time management strategies or systems that

you need to consider? If you ask ChatGPT to show you steps on how to organize your schedule, it's up to the task. It will show you something like:

- *"Making a list of tasks and events..."*
- *"Prioritize your tasks and events..."*
- *"Create a schedule..."*
- *"Be realistic about your time..."*
- *Review your schedule regularly..."*

This list is achievable, but you can ask it to be your assistant and give it a list of events and tasks that you want it to schedule over the course of a particular period.

Scheduling your Task

ChatGPT is capable of listing all your tasks on a daily and hourly basis. It's humane to schedule tasks because it intends to give you alternatives in case you get overwhelmed with a particular plan.

From my experience, I had included one gym session in my daily workout plan. But then I noticed that it had added two gym sessions instead. I queried the model's mistake, and then it made me understand that it wanted to provide me flexibility in case there's a clash in schedule or if I change my plans to work out at a different time. How smart!

According to a study that was conducted by economists at the Organization for Economic Co-operation and Development (OECD) about skills that AI could replicate, scheduling and prioritizing tasks was one of them. And you know what? The study picked "scheduling work and activities" as the "perfect AI problem."

Some workers are also automating their work schedules. Work doesn't have to drain the life out of you, you know. Just look at that.

Handle a Project Workflow

If you have a daunting project, ask ChatGPT to help organize it. It will consider the prompts that you put into consideration, which should include:

1. Tell ChatGPT the nature of the project that you intend to handle.

2. Ask for steps that you'll need to carry out this project, taking into consideration factors like deadlines and hours that you have to work on it.

3. You can set goals, create a budget, access information, and streamline communication within an organization with the help of ChatGPT. Using the ChatGPT Slack Integration, you're at liberty to ask ChatGPT questions and get responses directly from the Slack messaging platform. When you streamline your communication through the integration of ChatGPT with Slack. Using this automation, you can send a message straight from ChatGPT to Slack. Collaboration and teamwork sure get better and better.

It will do all of these things for you and save you hours of scheduling and preparation. You can also ask it to choose productivity apps that will help you go about your project, depending on what type it is. One such app is Rambox. It assists in setting reminders, managing your tasks, and remaining organized.

Other ways in which ChatGPT will assist you in managing your time effectively are:

1. By offering you reminders about a deadline that's

silently blinking somewhere in the corner of your mind. With useful features like task tracking, you can be sure nothing goes beyond your notice.

2. ChatGPT helps you create a to-do list. It's easy to get so carried away with a particular task that we forget that there's something else that needs to be done. ChatGPT will assist you in arranging your tasks in order of urgency after you send it a list of things that you hope to do on a particular day.

3. As a business owner, you can schedule meetings, track the progress of your projects, and organize your teams or individual tasks.

You'll see how much burden you'll let off yourself when you don't feel disorganized. I don't know if you can relate. But I feel fulfilled when I succeed at checking off every item on my to-do list. It's like a breath of fresh air. You can sit easily in your soapy bathtub after a long day and relax without your mind wandering toward something that you haven't done.

Collaborating with ChatGPT for Teamwork and Efficiency

In life, no one cares about the hurdles that you go through in the course of trying to achieve a goal. The only thing that people care about is the result.

You must have already seen how far you can go as an individual with ChatGPT. But as a team, it can be transformational. At this moment, not many people are aware of the fact that ChatGPT has been updated in such a way that you can work as a team using the model.

The left-hand side of your ChatGPT interface contains the

history of your conversations with the model. There's a share button. When you click on it, you can share a link with anyone on your team. And when they open the link, it will lead to the chat in that person's ChatGPT.

By implication, anything the other person adds to the chat becomes theirs, and you, the original owner, won't have it anymore. The advantage is that the chat history is safe and intact. Suppose there's a person on your team who's skilled at building a great conversation with the model and extracting useful information. In that case, it can be shared with other colleagues, and they can continue with the work without losing sight of the context that has been built.

Some organizations have a team member start with a particular prompt, after which AI does the rest of the work for them. Another team member cleans the extracted data to ensure that it's accurate and ready to share with the rest of the team as a single personalized ChatGPT.

But with ChatGPT, there's a strategy that you can consider. Here, someone on the team will build context and history from chats with the model, getting the ChatGPT right on track. Your history builder gives ChatGPT a role, offers some instructions and parameters, and then fine-tunes the model until it gets into the right frame. The customized ChatGPT is then sent to the team. Each team member can use their personalized ChatGPT with specific prompts to then receive answers tailored to each individual's needs. Finally, the history builder will compile, review, refine and clean up the responses before sharing them with the team.

Do you see how great this is for collaborations in the marketing space, or even the Human Resources department? As a prompt builder, this is a great opportunity for you to share your prompts with team members and even across departments in your organization. It's a potential business, don't you think? You could become a prompt builder who sells a personalized ChatGPT entity that you've built.

This is a great way for a marketing professional to organize ChatGPT for some SEO projects. It works well for different fields. In the prompt engineering space, the prompt building is a potential gold mine.

Streamlining Workflows with ChatGPT Integration

When workflows are streamlined, your work is well organized, which also ensures easy collaboration, as I explained earlier. Here's the "how" of streamlining workflows with ChatGPT integration:

- You can save a ChatGPT chat history for future reference and use AI automation to save it as a ClickUp comment.

- You can save your ChatGPT chat history. This is possible because the OpenAI automation helps you generate an essay in Google Docs, thereby streamlining the whole writing process.

- ChatGPT is great at shortening texts meant for platforms with character limits.

- It's a great grammar tool to correct and enhance your writing.

- It helps simplify complex concepts.

- ChatGPT can be used as a browser extension. This means that ChatGPT is on more than one screen and can perform various tasks depending on the extensions. It saves time in such a way that you don't have to keep going back and forth between tabs to get your work done.

There are different ways you can use and automate ChatGPT, thereby optimizing your workflow:

- You can generate an image from an email brief and send it to Slack. It will enhance visual communication.

- With ChatGPT, you can effortlessly formulate essays. With automation, you can generate an essay on Google Docs, making the writing process more streamlined.

- You can compose captivating tweets with the help of ChatGPT and save them directly on your Google Sheets. Watch your social media engagement management yield results through this strategy.

- Chatbot can enhance your outreach posts on LinkedIn. You get to generate personalized emails through this AI automation when you leverage the content of LinkedIn posts.

Once you begin incorporating these tips, you'll notice speed, efficiency, and accuracy. The level of your productivity will skyrocket, and you'll discover other ways of streamlining your workflow.

ChatGPT and Proactive Maintenance

Proactive maintenance (also called predictive maintenance) is a strategy geared towards identifying a problem and fixing irregularities behind the failure of equipment before it becomes a full-blown problem. It has been a topic of interest as organizations and management seek ways to optimize the management of their assets.

This strategy permits organizations to schedule maintenance activities based on data-driven insights instead of depending on fixed intervals or waiting for equipment to stop working. When a team submits inspection reports on equipment in the company, you can use ChatGPT to analyze the data and predict what maintenance strategy will be most suitable.

1. When you identify a potential problem and take steps, you schedule maintenance to ensure the longevity of the equipment. It's one of the benefits of using ChatGPT. It starts with processing and analyzing disorganized data. Unlike traditional data analysis, which struggles with unstructured data, ChatGPT has no problem evaluating it. With its natural language processing activities, it can draw valuable insights and provide a clear understanding of the state of the equipment and its performance.

2. ChatGPT helps team members share information more effectively by translating technical information that seems complex into clear language. It's a great tool for large organizations and maintenance teams that might not be in the same location. It ensures that each team member has access to the same information to collaborate easily on a maintenance task.

3. Another great benefit is that ChatGPT learns, adapts, and

updates itself. The more the AI model processes more data and gains a more in-depth understanding of equipment functions. It gets more accurate with its predictions and recommendations. It will ensure more efficient maintenance strategies.

4. Another advantage is that ChatGPT assists in inventory management and workforce planning. When the model provides adequate predictions, organizations can ensure that necessary spare parts and technical experts are available at the right time. It will further reduce maintenance costs while boosting operational effectiveness.

Staying Updated

ChatGPT, as a cutting-edge language model, stays updated with the latest trends and technologies in the chatbot industry. One of the key reasons it can remain current is its continuous training process with large amounts of text data. This training includes analyzing various sources such as news articles, blog posts, social media content, and technical publications related to chatbots.

For example, if a new breakthrough in natural language processing is published, ChatGPT's training process takes this into account and incorporates the knowledge into its responses. This ensures that the model is equipped with the latest advancements and can provide users with up-to-date information.

The team at OpenAI plays a crucial role in keeping ChatGPT relevant and accurate. They regularly review and update the model with the latest research findings and technological advancements. This constant monitoring and improvement process ensures that ChatGPT remains at the forefront of the chatbot industry.

Moreover, ChatGPT has the ability to learn from user interactions, which contributes to its adaptability and responsiveness. As more users interact with the model, it gains insights into new and emerging trends in real-world scenarios. This enables ChatGPT to evolve and provide more contextually appropriate answers over time.

For instance, if users frequently ask about a new chatbot platform or a trending chatbot feature, ChatGPT will recognize this pattern and incorporate the relevant information into its responses. As a result, users receive accurate and helpful insights on the latest developments in the chatbot industry.

By staying updated and learning from user interactions, ChatGPT can effectively provide valuable assistance in various domains. Whether it's offering customer support, providing information on the latest products and services, or assisting with creative writing, ChatGPT's ability to adapt and evolve ensures that it remains a valuable tool for users in an ever-changing chatbot landscape.

Troubleshooting and Support

We've sung the praises of ChatGPT since the beginning of this book about how revolutionary it is. But what happens when you're working on an important project and you get stuck? You turn to ChatGPT, and you notice that it's not working. You get frustrated, wondering what could have gone wrong. Here are some troubleshooting tips that could work for you if you're in this situation. First, what could be the reason for ChatGPT not working?

1. Server problems
As a tool that's cloud-based, if the servers are down or have technical glitches, you might not be able to access the model.

2. Poor Internet Connection
ChatGPT thrives on a stable internet connection. If your

internet is slow or fluctuating, you'll not have a smooth chatting experience with the model.

3. Technical Hiccups

Just like any other software, ChatGPT isn't immune to technical malfunctions. As a result, the tool might stop working or give inaccurate responses.

4. User Error

ChatGPT might be experiencing issues due to improper syntax in the prompt that the user added in the chats, leading to incorrect responses.

Now what's the way out of a ChatGPT hiccup?

1. **Check your internet connection.** If you discover that you're having connectivity issues, you can reboot your router or modem to stabilize your internet connection. If the problem continues, you can seek direction from your Internet Service Provider (ISP). They're capable of running a diagnosis and repairing any irregularity that might be affecting your internet connection.

2. **Check your login details.** Incorrect login details are a common cause of ChatGPT work errors. Double-check the information that you entered for your login.

3. **Refresh the page.** This will reload the tool and fix any technical irregularities or server issues. To refresh your page, click on the refresh button on your browser or press the shortcut key, F5. Doing this will reload the page. If nothing changes, clear your browser cache and cookies. It will evacuate any stored data that might constitute a problem for the tool. In addition, you can try accessing ChatGPT from a different device or browser to see if there'll be an improvement.

4. **Clean out your browser cache and cookies.** It will help remove corrupted files or data that might be affecting your ChatGPT experience. Many times, these temporary files are there to help websites load speedily. But they can accumulate over

time and cause performance issues for your tool. To clear your browser, go to your browser setting and find the option that says you should clear your browsing data. Choose the time range that you want to clear and the data type you would like to have removed like cookies and cache. After you're done, try reloading.

Note that if you're using a VPN connection, it might be blocking the common VPN IP addresses that your tool is using to prevent abuse. In this scenario, disconnecting the VPN connection might be the way out of your user problems with ChatGPT.

5. **Use a VPN.** If you're having network issues, using a Virtual Private Network might help you evade them. With a VPN, you can securely connect to the internet without experiencing any network impediments or firewalls that might be meddling with your tool. If you're using a VPN, choose a server close to your location to ensure speedy and optimized use of the internet. And if you're experiencing any network issues disconnect from the VPN to see if there's an improvement.

6. **Reach out to ChatGPT support.** If you've tried all that I mentioned earlier, and still have no improvement, contact the support team for guidance. They will help you troubleshoot the issue and find a solution. Visit their website and look out for the "Contact Us" section. Send an email, fill out a contact form, filling them in on the details of the problem.

You've sure come a long way. How has your experience been? Have you started implementing all that you've read so far? If you haven't, I want to believe that you got value and are getting ready to take action. You can be the best you can be in your personal and professional life.

6

ADVANCED TECHNIQUES AND STRATEGIES

"I am telling you, the world's first trillionaires are going to come from somebody who masters AI and all its derivatives and applies it in ways we never thought of."

— MARK CUBAN

ChatGPT has given search engines like Google, Yahoo, and Bing a run for their money. It all began somewhere. Before the advent of what we know today as the internet, there was something called 'cyberspace.' It was something that grew and developed with the evolution of science and technology. The foundation for the creation of science and technology was laid by individuals who saw the potential that information technology held. These were the ones sowing the seeds.

Our ability to access information at the snap of a finger wouldn't have been possible without folks like Vannevar Bush. Bush's writing was the first visionary depiction of the potential benefits of information technology through his description of the "memex" automated library system. Do you see the fore-shadowing of what we know today as ChatGPT?

The field of cybernetics was invented by Norbert Weiner, who inspired future researchers to be more fixated on the use of technology that would be aimed at extending human abilities. Do you remember the 1956 Dartmouth Artificial Intelligence Conference mentioned at the beginning? This was an event that further crystallized the idea that information technology was indeed advancing at an exponential rate.

What we know today as cyberspace encapsulates everything about the virtual world. It's something that we all experience in content and context. The virtual world can also be described as the internet, techno-world, cyber-world, electronic technology, information technology, and digital technology.

We discussed ways that we can make ChatGPT play the role that we want it to play. We can even trick it into giving responses that it wouldn't want to give for ethical reasons. But do you know you can customize the solutions you want ChatGPT to solve?

Do you know that you can make ChatGPT explore data outside its database? Do you know that the data in your ChatGPT doesn't need to have limited data to perform the tasks that you want it to perform?

This is where you get the drift.

Let's go.

Fine-tuning ChatGPT for Customized Solutions

A large language model (LLM) like ChatGPT is a natural language processing model that has been trained on a large amount of data to improve its ability to process language. The reason you might need to fine-tune the dataset in ChatGPT is to simply retrain it on a smaller and more domain-specific dataset.

It's the dataset that determines the quality of your output. The model becomes more intentional about the kind of information it'll reel out.

For example, if you're looking to work with data related to psychology, your language model needs to be retrained to be able to recognize any lexicon that's related to psychology. The model will not only understand the context. It'll also allow for smooth conversational flow.

You'll realize that the responses you get will be more precise and accurate. It can also match the kind of response that your organization requires. And you know the good thing? You won't need to go through the stress of retraining a model because you can reuse your models for specific use cases.

According to a recent research report by the MIT Technology Review, lack of quality data is the second greatest obstacle to engaging AI. As stated by Gartner (2023), it would be hard to feed the algorithms if there was no solid, clean data in large volumes.

In one of my favorite Sci-fi movies, Terminator, which portrays a dystopian society with AI robots bent on destroying humanity, the importance of data is brought to light. Arnold Schwarzenegger, who plays the Terminator, is programmed to hunt down and kill the hero, Sarah Connor. But the machine had no idea which Sarah Connor to target.

The only data that's left is her name and the city in which she lived. Without the slightest idea of his target, the Terminator had to rummage through a phone book, dispatching all the Sarah Connors he could find on the list. As intelligent as the Terminator is, it has to figure out the right Sarah Connor to target. Why is that? It's devoid of foundational training data. Eventually, after many sequels, the Terminator can fish out its target. Not until it was fed the appropriate training data through learning and fine-tuning.

It doesn't matter if it's a homicidal cyborg or a customer chatbot; AI needs the right data to make intelligent decisions and have conversations within its proper context.

How do you go about fine-tuning your ChatGPT?

First, you must be prepared with adequate data on the ground. Do you know the task that you have at hand? Are you knowledgeable enough about choosing the right dataset?

Let's begin with preparation. Anyone who wants to build a house must, first of all, count the cost. Get enough data related to the task ahead. The Terminator was only given a name and a city. He needed more than that to achieve that assignment. It's the same with you. Getting enough data will make your conversations with ChatGPT more personal. The model is more in touch with the conversation, and you get your desired output.

The next step is preprocessing and formatting. This requires that your dataset has a format that's compatible with ChatGPT. No digressions and no irrelevant information. Curating and properly formatting your data is the foundation and most important stage.

The next thing to do is to train ChatGPT. You have to set up the environment by installing the relevant libraries and tools that are required. What are the hyperparameters that determine the training process? They include learning rate, batch size, and number of training sessions. Learning rate can be defined as how fast your network transitions from a learned familiar concept to something new.

For example, when a kid continues to get fed milk, he or she might think or believe that milk is the only food. Now, when a child is shown various kinds of meals like Pizza, he or she moves on from that thought and understands that milk is not the only food. With a low learning rate, a kid might consider that Pizza is an outlier and continue to believe that milk is the only food. And if the learning rate is super high, the kid would instantly believe that milk is not the only meal and that Pizza and other kinds of meals can be enjoyed. So, a model that has a good learning rate will present state-of-the-art results.

Batch size has to do with the number of images used to train a single forward and backward pass. It has a direct impact on the accuracy and efficiency of the training process. Decreasing the batch rate helps the network train better when it comes to fine-tuning. When a batch size is large, the training process can be fast but can lead to overfitting and low accuracy. Meanwhile, smaller batch sizes give room for accuracy but can be pretty expensive.

The number of training sessions, which can also be called an epoch, is the number of times that the whole dataset has to be worked on or tested through the learning algorithm.

Now, after considering these parameters, we move on to the next, which is feeding the curated data into ChatGPT. This is how the model learns from the dataset that you've provided. Ensure that you closely monitor the training process. If you feel like it's not meeting your expectations, it's okay to adjust the parameters.

The next thing to do is to fine-tune the code that you would like to use. This stage requires that you feed the formatted dataset into the code. This code fine-tunes ChatGPT for the dataset.

You need to be careful to keep each record smaller than 2048 tokens. After your dataset is ready, run it through the OpenAI command-line tool to authorize it. The command is: Openaitools fine_tunes. Prepare_data-<LOCAL _FILE>

It's okay to pass files in CSV, TSV, XLSX, JSON, or JSONL format to this tool. It will help you convert it into a dataset that's ready to be fine-tuned.

To train a new, fine-tuned model, you need to run the command below to train the model that you've just fine-tuned:

Openai api fine_tunes.create-t
<TRAIN_FILE_ID_OR_PATH>-m
<BASE_MODEL>

Replace the file name and base model name with the training dataset and GPT model that you would love your training to be based on.

Evaluate the fine-tuned model to be sure that it's working perfectly. If there's a need to adjust the fine-tuning technique or hyperparameters, you can do so. You're free to also repeat the process if need be.

These are the four fine-tuning techniques that you can consider.

Few-shot learning: This technique refers to fine-tuning with a small amount of data. It comes in handy when you've got labeled data restricted for the task ahead.

Zero-shot learning: With this technique, you fine-tune ChatGPT for a task that it has never been trained for.

Continual learning: This requires the continuous feeding of ChatGPT with new information over time as new data is released. The aim is to keep the model updated, accurate, and relevant.

Multi-Task Learning: ChatGPT can be fine-tuned on different related tasks simultaneously. It will be great for those who want to optimize their ChatGPT to handle different tasks.

ChatGPT isn't only a role player. It's a sort of search engine that you can mold to give you the kind of data that you want. It's also your search engine.

Exploring External Knowledge Sources for Enriched Responses

Information is so readily available, like noodles or microwaved food. You need not go too far these days. Despite the limited data in the knowledge base of ChatGPT, you can make data available to ChatGPT. We're rich with information through Wiki pages at work, company knowledge, Google documents, Reddit, newsletters, etc. Keeping up with these pieces of information can be daunting. So what's the way out?

Simple!

You can choose where to extract your data and feed ChatGPT with the information. You're the boss, right? You don't have to be bound by pieces of information that the model has been trained on.

Sometimes you just want to interact with the model about something the public isn't aware of. It could be some top business secret that you don't want leaked.

There are moments when you want large-sized PDFs, datasheets, emails, and database entries.

You also don't want ChatGPT to assume facts. You want your model to strictly focus on your data and honestly reveal that it doesn't have any idea about a particular concept by saying something like, *"Sorry, I'm not aware of this information."*

What about those times when you would need a direct reference to the source of information that it has used to provide an answer?

In all of these scenarios, how do you explore external sources to incorporate into ChatGPT?

I give it what I have

You can incorporate the entire data into the ChatGPT prompt. In cases like this, it's easy for ChatGPT to read the data in its proper context and respond accordingly. There would be no need to retrain or fine-tune. The advantage of this method is that it can easily adapt to any alterations in the base data. However, there's a constraint. When it comes to context length, there's a limit to what the model can take. Even without constraints, it won't make that much sense to flood large gigabytes of data into a text prompt for every conversation.

Storing what I have

Another technique for exploring external data sources in a database outside the model is easy retrieval at times when you might need it.

There are a lot of possibilities when it comes to creating prompts, extracting data from a knowledge base, crafting queries, and coordinating the conversational language between ChatGPT and the knowledge base. Let's look at some potential tactics that can be applied:

1. Ask ChatGPT to transform the user input (including chat history) into a specific query, which is your knowledge base.

For example, a user could ask, *"Which year had the highest growth in tech stocks?"* In this step, the GPT model (which can use any of the GPT-3 models like text-DaVinci, text curie, and so on.) will receive a question that's more modified, like, *"I have my data stored in the ABC database. My user is asking, "Which year had the highest growth in tech stocks?" Please convert this question into a data query from my database."*

2. You can use the data query from the first step to get all the relevant information in your data storage. The information chunks could be in the form of PDF sections, emails, or files that are related to yearly sales by revenue. The chunks will be sorted or arranged in order of relevance.

3. Feed the information chunks that you've just accessed to the ChatGPT and request that it use them as context in answering the main question.

4. In our example, ChatGPT will get a modified question

again, like: *"My user asks me 'which year had the highest growth in tech stocks' Please answer that question with the information provided here...*

Answer: 'I don't know' if none of the available data has a specific answer to the user question."

Other data sources can be financial reports, sales data, interaction logs, or any form of structured or unstructured data. After identifying the sources of your data, the first major step has to be preparing your data for effective querying. This involves cleaning and normalizing the data, eliminating any irrelevant information, and converting the data into a format that's text-based so that both the data query and ChatGPT can easily comprehend it.

At times, your data might chat with real people through emails or instant messaging. Think about eliminating all the traces of email formalities like, "Dear Xyz, Kind regards, Ben". These are irrelevant and can potentially pollute the data.

You can consider splitting the data inputs for easy reference and proper citations. For example, you can split PDF files into a one-page document, helping you to make suitable citations (You might ask the model to take you to the exact page where the data was extracted from). After this, you can process each page independently, extracting the texts and tables and chunking them into different corresponding sections. One of the tools that could be useful for this is the Recursive Character Text Splitter from the LangChain library.

You need to add domain-relevant context to the conversation. Don't expect ChatGPT to understand the domain with just a few brief questions. Consider adding domain-relevant context to the questions. Provide descriptions of what the model should and shouldn't respond to, and tell it how to go about formatting responses. For example, you can create a ChatGPT-based therapist assistant and enter the input with an explanation like, *"You're an automated assistant to a therapist. Your user (a therapist) is attending to a client. Please answer the following questions using the data below..."*

It has been proven over time that conversational context such as this makes ChatGPT more accurate and precise, making it easy to produce enough relevant responses.

Using ChatGPT for Predictive Analysis and Forecasting

In the business world, one way to stay on top, and ahead is to be proactive. One of the magic touches and revolutionary moves of ChatGPT is its ability to predict and forecast through the power of natural language processing (NLP). As a cloud-based platform, it enables users to engage with data in natural language. It will make it easier to gain insights and make decisions intelligently. Through a merge of NLP and machine learning, ChatGPT understands the context of user queries and generates accurate predictions.

Just so you'll know, predictive analytics has transformed from a luxury to a necessity. It has become the secret weapon that sets successful digital marketers apart from their peers (Karthik, 2023). Predictive analytics allows users to detect patterns in their data and make predictions about trends based on their observations. With this, businesses can make better decisions and be steps ahead of the competition. Knowledge about what could happen in the future will inspire businesses to plan.

Now, businesses can smell the coffee. They're reducing costs and increasing profit. Using AI-powered algorithms, ChatGPT can process large amounts of data to predict sales trends, customer behavior, and market trends. Your business can gain insight into customer behavior, making you more aware of customer needs. You can know the potential risks of a certain type of business, and make the right decisions about marketing and product development. Analyzing data from different sources is a flexible feature of ChatGPT (Frąckiewicz, 2023).

If you're looking to invest in stocks, who says you can't forecast stock price movements with ChatGPT? You should wonder if it can. According to research conducted by Lopez-Lira and Yuehua (2023) on ChatGPT's ability to forecast stock market movement, they found that basic models like GPT-1, GPT-2, and BERT lack the accuracy to forecast returns effectively. However, complex models like ChatGPT-4 demonstrate the emerging capacity to predict returns with higher implied Sharpe ratios compared to ChatGPT-3. Despite this, ChatGPT-3 still achieves larger total returns.

According to them, integrating advanced language models like ChatGPT into investment decision-making processes can lead to more precise predictions and improved performance in quantitative trading strategies. Notably, predictability is more prominent in smaller stocks and firms with negative news, suggesting the presence of limits-to-arbitrage rather than market inefficiencies.

Incorporating Reinforcement Learning for Optimal Results

I see reinforcement learning as something similar to learning on the job. One of the reasons ChatGPT has remained undefeated since its release is due to its training technique, which is reinforcement learning from human feedback (RLHF). Reinforcement learning is a field of machine learning in which an agent becomes conversant with a policy through its interactions with its environment.

First, the agent gets into action, which could include not doing anything at all. The action affects the environment in which the agent lives, which switches to a new state and brings about a reward.

Rewards are the feedback signs that help the reinforcement learning (RL) agent adjust its action policy or guidelines. The more training the agent goes through, the more policy changes there are.

ChatGPT uses reinforcement learning from human feedback in a phase called model fine-tuning. Through mimicking, reinforcement learning agents mimic and predict how humans speak to each other daily. It includes the specific language used as well as syntax and diction.

Reinforcement learning comprises three steps:

1. **Supervised Fine-Tuning (SFT)**: This is a pre-trained model fine-tuned on a small amount of demonstrated data curated by labelers to understand and learn a supervised policy that generates output from a specific list of prompts.

2. **Imitate human preferences**: Labelers are required to vote on a large number of the SFT model outputs. This is how a new dataset is generated, comprising comparison data. A new model is trained on this particular dataset. It's called the reward model (RM).

3. **Proximal Policy Optimization**: The reward model is utilized to further fine-tune and upgrade the SFT model. The result of this step is called the policy model.

The first step happens only once, while the second and third can be adjusted repeatedly. More comparison data is gathered on the existing best policy model, used to train a fresh reward model and then an updated policy.

ChatGPT goes through reinforcement learning to get fine-tuned, using human feedback in the training loop to cut off any harmful or biased output.

Combining ChatGPT with other AI tools for Synergistic Effects

Surfing through the net, you'll notice that many influencers are talking about other AI tools that can handle tasks alongside Chat-GPT. ChatGPT has been the talk of the town quite a bit, and it's worth the hype. But it's not all-inclusive. It can't do everything. Do you want to know the things it can't do that other AI tools can? Here it is:

- ChatGPT is trained on data. So it can't generate new or real-time data.

- It can't generate visual or AI arts.

- It can't accept voice commands or generate vocal responses.

- When using ChatGPT, add-ons like Instagram, Twitter, Gmail, etc. aren't available.

- ChatGPT alternatives provide options to generate factual articles or blogs that are specialized, customized, and brand-specific on the latest topics, which is a major requirement for any kind of business.

- Unlike other AI models, ChatGPT doesn't have a no-code AI chatbot solution that can easily integrate into websites and attend to inquiries in real-time.

All the more reason to combine ChatGPT with other AI tools to make up for those limitations.

As a business, you can use ChatGPT with automation to conduct repetitive tasks more productively and smartly. Just as Microsoft is integrating AI into Teams to boost features like minute-taking, AI can be combined with chatbots to make them much smarter if they're trained properly on the right datasets.

Another AI tool that has stormed the tech space is Midjourney. Midjourney is a tool that focuses on creating visuals that seem like real moments frozen in time. For this AI tool to unleash its potential, it needs the right prompts. This can prove challenging, but ChatGPT can do the work for you. You start by feeding ChatGPT. It helps in creating Midjourney prompts. But it needs all the necessary information. The moment it's fed with the appropriate prompts, you'll find yourself creating one of the most beautiful works of art you've ever seen.

Step 1: You can ask ChatGPT for a prompt for the art generator. *"Please provide a prompt that can be used by a generative art software like Midjourney that would lead to having cool imagery of an astronaut cat?"*

This is what ChatGPT came back with: *"Create a captivating artwork of an astronaut cat exploring the cosmos. Showcase the feline astronaut in a futuristic space suit, surrounded by celestial wonders and distant galaxies."*

Step 2: Copy these results and clean or adjust them accordingly before pasting them into Midjourney AI or other AI generative art programs, then wait for the result. You'll be amazed at the incredible results.

Other AI tools are:

1. **Rewind AI** – We could call this a search engine for your life. Have you ever scrolled through the internet and forgotten everything that you were looking at? But you manage to remember one keyword. Then you have to go through your

history. If it's a video, you try to figure out at what point that statement was made. This tool helps you search for what someone told you or what you watched in a particular video and find it so you don't have to struggle to remember everything. This will help many people improve their productivity because there are so many things calling for our attention nowadays.

2. **Runway** – You can use this AI tool to edit videos and images. You can even expand your images with this tool. You can change the background of a photo, change the frame, change objects in a picture, clean your audio, and perform motion tracking.

3. **Pictory** – This AI tool is used to create videos just by uploading text. It's quite great for content creators. You can edit videos using text, edit visuals, and upload articles. Pictory AI can provide a video for that article by just reading the text. Scripts can be turned into videos as well. It's a story-telling app.

4. **Reword** – Rather than responding to prompts, you can train the AI with your existing articles. Since AI-generated content lacks the opinion and creativity of a human writer, Reword improves on this by asking you to prime the AI by giving you information about your readers and what you write about generally. There's a provision for you to upload examples of your writing manually. Now, this is where Reword shows up. Connect it to the Google Search Console (GSC). When connected to GSC, it understands the search intent behind your articles and analyzes click-through rates, which is a badass feature if you're trying to grow an online blog. The writing interface is great, too. As for the UX, it's simple. You can brainstorm titles and sections for your article on the right side of the bar, and Reword will provide a selection of suggested titles and sections for you to select from, which reduces the time you would have spent researching. You get to enjoy three AI buttons- AI enriches, AI rephrases, and AI shortens. It also has an AI command, which

leads to a window where you can enter prompts or utilize templates.

There are so many AI tools that you can use as support tools for whatever tasks you would like to carry out.

Pushing the Boundaries: Research and Development Opportunities

Here, we're talking about pushing the boundaries through the use of AI tools. When we talk about a revolution, it means something is no longer according to the status quo. The lines are beginning to blur. AI is creating both written and video content and even getting acknowledged for it in clear writing. As much as it has presented challenges, it has also presented opportunities.

When it comes to research, it has left room for advancement in data science due to the exponential growth of big data. Data has begun to transform itself into the most important and indispensable asset for any organization.

With the advancement of science and technology and the high demand for data-driven insights, data science has steadily evolved. In recent times, trends in the field have included the increased popularity of artificial intelligence and machine learning. There's also the rise of cloud computing, big data, the common use of data visualization tools, and of course, ChatGPT.

For programmers, ChatGPT is a valuable resource as they improve their skills and scale their coding challenges. If you're someone who doesn't know Jack about programming, you can create workable code on your own. Are you seeking explanations and examples of programming concepts such as algorithms, data structures, syntax, and so much more? ChatGPT is the model that would be of immense benefit. As you've seen, ChatGPT has not ceased to redefine the limitations that are used to govern what a machine can learn.

Now that the world has seen the influence of ChatGPT on society, other tech giants like Google are working toward creating their own version of the model. Google's Bard is being further developed. The more time and investment that flow into research and development related to this field, the higher our expectations will be for new models that are much more sophisticated. There'll come a time when these models will carry out data science related tasks that are more complex and refined.

Opportunities abound in ChatGPT for those who want to spend most of their lives as researchers. If this is you, you have a great supporter in your writing process, even providing research ideas. It'll help you spend more time experimenting and implementing your findings. Since ChatGPT summarizes texts, you have no problem understanding a published work that you need as a reference.

I must admit that educators are in one of the best times of their lives. ChatGPT is a tool that can help educators create lesson plans for any kind of course, be it computer science, physics, civil engineering, psychology, philosophy, and so on. To allow easy understanding, some educators might need illustrations, activities, and topic-specific exercises. ChatGPT is also used to generate quiz questions that are custom-made to the subject matter and level of difficulty of the course.

Educators have also gotten personalized learning support for students. ChatGPT can provide customized resources depending on a student's needs and learning style. For instance, if you're looking to evaluate the student performance data to analyze areas where a student might be struggling, ChatGPT can help you with that. Just provide enough data from your observations.

Innovations in Natural Language Processing and ChatGPT's Future

NLP is a field of computer science that's about understanding, analyzing, and generating natural language. The beauty of it is its application to other professional fields like health, entertainment, education, and so on.

A major and most common NLP task is sentiment analysis, which tries to identify and deduce attitude and emotional tone. As someone who wants to be aware of customers' feedback, preferences, opinions, and an understanding of your social media presence and brand reputation, you should run a sentimental analysis. What are the innovations that have gradually seeped into this field? There's a fine-grained analysis that can detect not just the tone of a text but the aspect, intensity, and target of the sentiment. Also, there's a multi-modal analysis that combines text with other modalities like images, audio, or videos to capture the entire sentiment, and a cross-lingual analysis that can take care of texts in different cultural contexts and languages.

Text summarization, which is another task in NLP, has also experienced changes. We have abstractive summarization that can create summaries that aren't limited by the phrases in the original text but can rephrase, reword, paraphrase, or even provide new information. And with the introduction of extractive summarization, you can choose the most relevant phrases and sentences from the original text and convert them into a summary.

NLP has been able to respond accurately to natural language questions. But it has broken the limits of the domain. It can handle any question from any topic or field by extracting answers from a large and varied collection of sources, like the web, knowledge graphs, or databases. NLP can easily maintain a conversation with an understanding of the context of each query that's thrown at it through handling follow-up questions, feedback, or clarification. NLP has also upgraded to visual question answering; that is, it can respond to questions that demand an understanding of text and images like photos, charts, or diagrams.

As a model that has made its mark in different fields, you can't deny that ChatGPT has revolutionized different fields. It has unlocked new horizons in artificial intelligence and transformed different aspects of society in the process. Are you thinking about what the future holds concerning this AI model? Here's how to know:

- In the healthcare system, medical professionals have found a way to evaluate and diagnose patient conditions.

- In the entertainment industry, it can generate intriguing storylines for movies, and TV shows, and push the boundaries of fun and creativity.

- Businesses can make informed decisions based on insights and forecasts carried out on the model through analysis of vast amounts of data.

- More careers will be born. There's no point in whining about AI taking over jobs. Organizations are keenly looking out for individuals who have an understanding of ChatGPT. Did you know that prompt building is a potential career in the career world?

To remain relevant and productive in the area of technology, you need to flow with the times. According to Neumann (2023), in the near future, people who know how to utilize AI tools will be more efficient than those who don't because ChatGPT will play the role of an assistive tool for them. Furthermore, he asserts that it's best that people accept this game changer that has impacted our daily lives.

Exploring ChatGPT's Potential in Voice and Multimodal Interfaces

Recently, I read about someone who set up a voice interface to ChatGPT for his 3-year-old kid and was impressed by its results. This shows that there remains a future for interactions with chatbots.

Okay, what does the term "multimodal" mean in the context of artificial intelligence?

AI simply can function in multiple modes or capacities, which include text, images, and sound. Through DALL-E or ChatGPT, interactions with humans were only restricted to text inputs. With the release of GPT-4, there's room for speech, images, and video as input, and to provide text-based answers.

Applications of multimodal interfaces can understand and transcribe spoken language, interpret visual data, and understand written texts. It's not restricted to one mode. It can combine inputs from different modalities to understand a given situation.

With the integration of ChatGPT with some other AI technologies like speech recognition, and computer vision, there will be unhindered communication between humans and machines. When I combined Midjourney AI with ChatGPT, I was in awe of the integration of written text into an image-creating AI model.

Multimodal interactions save the user's time and effort. It

also makes technology easier to use and access for those who find the traditional interfaces difficult to use.

When it comes to unlocking the potential of ChatGPT's voice technology, there has been a revolution in the way humans interact with machines. This has given hope to those living with disabilities. The key features of ChatGPT's AI voice technology are the following:

1. It can be integrated into other technologies like machine learning, natural language processing, and voice recognition.

2. Developers access ChatGPT, allowing them to use voice technology in their applications.

3. ChatGPT voice technology can be executed through different programming languages, such as Python and JavaScript.

4. It can also be used to power voiceovers, offering natural human speech for text-to-speech and video content.

The voice technology of ChatGPT can be integrated into email services like Gmail, integrated with other voice assistants, served as a learning resource, integrated into IoT (Internet of Things) devices, used for real-time translation, used by game developers to create non-playable characters, and so on. The list goes on. Voice technology has broken all limits. It can be integrated into services, applications, and systems.

PART III

___

OPTIMIZATION FOR IMPROVED PRODUCTIVITY

This is the part where we discuss how you can save your personal information and boost your business while you use ChatGPT. This isn't the time to become a doomsday proclaimer. It's high time you smelled the coffee, strapped your belt, and got ready to flow with change. You can grow to lord it over AI, not the other way around. This last part is rich with so much information. Knowledge sets you apart, and you don't want to rush the process.

Come with me.

7

OPTIMIZATION TECHNIQUES

"The world is changing very fast. Big will not beat small anymore. It will be the fast beating the slow"

— RUPERT MODUCH

Are you familiar with being in a situation where you think, *"I knew this was too good to be straightforward?"* This reminds me of Mathematics classes. The teacher would give straightforward examples, and then you would think you're on top of the world. Then the teacher would assign you more complex questions for classwork and assignments compared to the simple classwork. Unfair, right?

I will call those days my first taste of disillusionment.

These are the moments when you finally realize that there's more to something than just looking at it at face value. It could be a person, a group, or even an investment. There's more to every great innovation.

There's more to ChatGPT than catches the eye. However, this isn't to portray it as anything less than hype, but to let you know that, just like the humans that created it, it's nothing near perfect. It's a groundbreaking innovation that's still developing.

Now, with the imperfection of ChatGPT, you need to ask questions like:

How do I manage this AI model efficiently?

How do I detect content that's AI-generated?

How do I know if a particular piece of content, like statistics, is accurate?

How do I deal with bias and controversial outputs from ChatGPT?

Those questions are necessary if you want to get the most from this AI model. Well, your curiosity will not linger for too long because I've curated answers to those questions and spread them into sections in this chapter. You just found your answers. Now let's read.

Continuous Training and Improvement

ChatGPT improves as you feed it with data. This is how you get it to advance. The ability of ChatGPT to learn, become smarter, and have intelligent conversations is made possible by a method called Transfer Learning (Kanade, 2022). This gives it the ability to transfer knowledge from one task to another. Since the goal of AI is to reason and make decisions like humans, it needs to learn from its experiences and adapt to any changes. This is where continuous learning comes into play. ChatGPT adapts to new experiences through different forms of exposure. By making data available for learning from and using in decision-making, it is made possible. It further gets conditioned as time goes by.

Every experience you have with the AI model through your chat history is a lesson for the machine. Its transformer-based architecture allows machines to learn over time. As a result, you begin to have more natural and intelligent conversations.

What other things do you hope to achieve when ChatGPT goes through continuous learning and improvement?

- Conversations become more meaningful.

- ChatGPT begins to understand the language, and the lexicon attached to your data becomes sharper. It will also learn how to respond to different contexts.

A study from the University of California revealed that when a model is exposed to large amounts of data from conversations, it becomes more effective. The improvement of the model was in its accurate responses to prompts and its ability to maintain context. As a virtual assistant or automated customer service agent, ChatGPT can deliver if trained. It has even set the pace for new possibilities in the health, finance, and education sectors.

Monitoring AI-Generated Content

A professor once spoke about how impressed he was with a particular student's write-up. But then he got more apprehensive when he saw the student's name. It couldn't be. This particular student, for most of the semester, has been consistent in submitting wishy-washy assignments. What could have happened? *"This improvement is too sudden,"* he thought. The next day, he called the student aside during break to defend his assignment. His experience with this student led him to learn about AI-generated content.

What's AI-generated content? AI-generated content is any kind of content generated with the help of machine learning algorithms or other AI tools (McKinsey, 2023). It got more popular after the launch of ChatGPT.

You can attest to the fact that generating content has gotten much easier and has become more accessible. It's not surprising to see an increase in the creation of AI-generated content. And this includes written texts, images, and videos. It's constantly used by businesses, marketers, and individuals to streamline production and automate content creation. Despite this, there's a need to distinguish between the content created by humans and the one created by AI. This need has become important in fields like journalism, education, art, medicine, and social media.

For instance, in a field like journalism, the spread of fake news generated by AI can cause significant damage to society. In the arts and humanities, an AI-generated artwork can raise questions about the integrity of a work and cause cynicism even when a text is human-made and original. In the education sector, it can raise issues of plagiarism. In the medical world, wrong assumptions or statistics about a disease can be an issue of life and death.

In light of this, the innovation of tools to detect AI-generated content has become necessary to put things in check. There's also a need to create and improve these AI-detecting tools to ensure the credibility and authenticity of the content. It will also solve the issues of plagiarism and academic integrity.

Stylometry is a technique to monitor the authenticity of content. Basically, it is employed to analyze and detect if a writing style is AI or human. This technique involves analyzing the patterns in the use of language, even the vocabulary, grammar, and syntax, to know the mind behind the text and determine the authorship. It can decipher the authorship of a text from the writing style (Gomez Adorno et al., 2018).

Another technique for detecting AI content is the use of metadata. This comprises information or details about the text, ranging from the device used to generate the content, the time it was created, and the date of creation (Bang and Woo, 2021).

Other online tools used to detect AI-generated content include Copyleaks and Turnitin.

Apart from techniques, there are also styles used to detect AI-generated content. One such tool is the GPT Output Detector. This tool helps analyze texts that are rifted for any patterns that indicate that particular content was generated by ChatGPT.

There's also an AI-detecting tool called Dungeon Detector. This tool is used for analyzing any text generated by the AI Dungeon to determine if it was created by a human or an AI. AI Dungeon is a tool that's used to generate interactive stories. This particular tool is based on statistical models and heuristics that evaluate different features of the stories, like the language, plot structure, and how coherent the narrative is. It ensures that everything in the storyline adds up. You don't want a storyline that says the main character is Michael Jackson and the story ends up being a Mary J. Blige story for the most part.

Another tool for detecting AI-generated content is TELLER. TELLER was developed by researchers at the University of California to distinguish between an image generated by humans and one generated by AI. Some of the things that the tool analyzes are color distribution, texture, and spatial arrangement.

Fakespot is an AI-detecting tool that's used to identify fake or biased reviews that might have been generated by AI. It analyzes the features of the reviews, using a machine-learning algorithm. Some of the features that it reviews include the use of language, the emotions expressed, and the reviewers' histories. I guess, these days, you can't judge the quality of a product by its reviews. You've just got to risk using a product or following your instincts. And if you want to go the extra mile, these tools will be just right for you.

Do you want to be sure about the authenticity of an image? You've got Truepic to help you out. TruePic will help you detect any form of manipulation or alteration in a photograph. It analyzes features like compression artifacts, pixel distribution, and metadata to deduce if the media has been altered or tampered with in any way.

If you want to go into the academic world, try as much as possible to channel your smarts toward the effective use of technology to achieve academic excellence. Copyscape is a plagiarism detection software that will be of immense help to you. It will help search the internet for any content that might be similar to the one that's being analyzed. If you're a blogger or website owner, you might need to be sure that your content is original.

Turnitin is a plagiarism detection software used by universities and professors to analyze papers to check for plagiarism. The papers of students are compared to a large database of web sources and academic sources.

There are a lot more of them that you can explore. However, these tools come with limitations. I don't think I've found any technology that didn't come with a counter-technology. It's like a Tom and Jerry narrative.

For example, if you want to use metadata to analyze content, the analysis might not be reliable if the metadata has been altered. Stylometry might not be accurate with its analysis because a model might have been trained to mimic the stylistics of human writing.

The significance of being able to detect AI-generated content will help enforce academic integrity, preventing the spread of fake news that will cause harm to society, and ensuring that artists are given the credit that they deserve. Being able to use these tools also ensures that academic integrity remains a core value in our higher institutions and that those in academia are given the credit and acknowledgement that they deserve.

Social media went agog after the voices of artists were placed on songs that weren't sung by them originally. If the people weren't aware of the song right from when it was released, they could have sworn the song was for them. They sounded so good. Imagine hearing Whitney Houston's voice on a Rihanna song. It's laughable, right? But then, it's possible. And it happened right before our eyes. That's one of the superpowers of AI.

There's another angle to this. This is an aspect of ethical considerations in terms of intellectual property and privacy. If AI-generated content is created using private data like personal emails or social media posts, detecting that content will be an infringement on a person's privacy rights.

Let's look at the commercial angle. If AI-generated content is used to promote or advertise a brand, detecting the content might have repercussions regarding intellectual property rights.

To balance the need for progress and improvement in the field of AI with the ethical concerns linked to detecting AI-generated content, transparency and accountability are necessary. Developers of these AI-detecting tools should be transparent about the techniques for detecting AI-generated content.

Quality Assurance Techniques for Accuracy and Relevance

The idea of ensuring accuracy and relevance is enforced in education, academics, and even visual space. There have been reports about the inaccuracies in the answers given by ChatGPT. One of them is unveiled in the experience of Needleman (2023), who was trying to test the ChatGPT in the Operation Management Course. On the one hand, the results showed that ChatGPT had learned basic operations management and process analysis questions. But on the other hand, it made serious errors with simple calculations in 6th-grade mathematics.

After a study on assessing the accuracy of ChatGPT through the principles of statistics exam, Al-Quadri and Ahmed (2023) were able to conclude that every piece of information from

ChatGPT needs to be cross-referenced before making any major decision.

The study was accompanied by some recommendations to improve performance on the questions related to the principles of statistics. These suggestions also apply to other aspects, be they finance, education, content creation on social media, or journalism. Here they are:

- There's a need to increase the diversity of the training data to include a wider variety of concepts and different types of problems.

- There should be a real-time assessment of the model to give its responses some feedback, especially questions that were accurately answered.

- To monitor the advancement of the model and discover opportunities for upgrading, it needs to be regulated regularly using a wide range of prompts.

- Incorporating learning strategies needs to be integrated, permitting the model to ask for clarification or extra information to understand the question better.

- You can utilize learning strategies that are hinged on new technologies to assist students in achieving their goals in the modern world.

- Modern assessment methods should be considered to avoid cheating in online teaching exams and achieve transparency.

There are a lot of things that ChatGPT can't do, but humans can. As a researcher, you need to be aware of these limitations and the unique abilities only humans have. When you work in conjunction with the model, you won't see the need to be too dependent on it to advance the need for research.

Integrating ChatGPT with Existing Systems and Workflows

Based on Gartner's study, 70% of organizations have begun exploring different ways of integrating AI into their daily operations (Egham, 2019).

Did you also know that Grand View Research projects the global AI market to reach a massive $733.7 billion by 2027? To top it all, it keeps growing at a compound annual rate of 42.2% (Frąckiewicz, 2023). These staggering statistics only portray the rapid adoption of AI. And of course, ChatGPT is blinking steadily at the center of this technological revolution.

From automating customer service and content creation to enhancing data analysis, and personalization, integrating ChatGPT is fast proving to be the new tactic for many businesses who want to stay ahead and relevant in the market and among their competitors.

Getting the most out of ChatGPT requires providing outputs aligned with your business or enterprise. Integrating AI tools into your structure is not a walk in the park. But if the right infrastructure isn't implemented, a business could get relegated to the background. You'll fail to realize the potential of your business and get stuck in inefficient processes if you don't unlock AI capabilities. You need sophisticated integration methods that can govern and incorporate any AI that has existing systems.

You already know that traditional software development cycles are slow and time-consuming, which could quell your sense of innovation. You need to deploy AI services in your work-flows and decision-making.

You can't just use ChatGPT in your enterprise. It should be integrated into it based on your company/business' unique data. If you pose questions like *"When do I get to go on leave?"* to Chat-GPT, you might get generic answers from internet-based training data, which might be accurate but won't be tailored to the context of your employer's needs.

If your ChatGPT is to be effective, it needs to obtain company-specific knowledge. This is to understand the context of a request and to ensure security because not every piece of information should be accessible to all employees.

Integrating ChatGPT is more than just plugging it in. Businesses need to be sure that their data is secure. They need to be able to interact with current systems in real-time to provide accurate and contextual responses in just about any format. If a response or conversation has to involve third parties, the model should do so in a similar context. It's how everyone in the organization understands the narrative and works toward achieving a goal.

There are requirements and considerations that businesses should make while trying to build a secure and productive AI environment.

A business should obtain AI tools to optimize workflows and improve business processes. Incorporating these solutions into real-time systems can be daunting.

ChatGPT integration involves integrating ChatGPT into different applications, systems, and platforms to offer advanced language understanding and the ability to generate effectively.

With the advent of machine learning technologies and AI, this integration has begun to change how businesses operate, opening doors of opportunity. Due to this, businesses are quickly introducing ChatGPT into their products and services.

The transformer architecture, which is at the core of Chat-GPT, uses unsupervised learning to train on a vast amount of data. Having this foundation enables ChatGPT to predict the next word about to come after a sentence. It bases its predictions on the context provided by the preceding words.

Interactive conversations are possible with the model by storing the conversation history and extending it with every new user's message and response to the model.

To customize the behavior of ChatGPT, you can fine-tune parameters like temperature and max tokens. With higher temperature values, the output will be more innovative and unpredictable. As for the max tokens parameter, it's about managing the length of the texts generated.

Here are different ways in which ChatGPT integration works.

- It powers virtual assistants and chatbots to be intelligent, providing 24-hour customer support daily, reducing response time, and boosting the customer experience.

- It can handle an endless number of interactions. It comes in handy when there's an upsurge in demands and inquiries.

- Costs are reduced when you automate tasks that are traditionally performed by humans.

- The experience with your users gets more personalized.

- It gets even easier to analyze user feedback or social media posts. This offers helpful insights into customer sentiment.

At this point, you say, "*Yeah, I get it. How do I go about it?*"

This isn't a problem. To integrate ChatGPT into your systems, applications, or platforms, you would use ChatGPT's API. It involves the following steps:

Step 1: The first step requires that you set up your environment. To achieve this, you should install the OpenAI Python client, which offers a Python interface to the OpenAI API.

Step 2: After the first step, you need to have an access key to the OpenAI API. This can be gotten from their website.

Step 3: You then send a prompt to the AI. The prompt could be messages with roles, such as 'user', 'system', or 'assistant', and queries. 'System' is used to establish the behavior of the assistant, 'user' is for inputs or prompts, and 'assistant' is for the response of the model.

Step 4: The moment the prompt has been sent, the API gives back a generated message.

Step 5: This is the part where you fine-tune the behavior of the model by tweaking parameters, such as the temperature (that controls impulsiveness) and max tokens (that controls length).

The major benefit of using OpenAI's API for integration is the high-quality customization that it provides. However, it requires some level of technical expertise.

If you have a business and you're seeking a quicker and ready-made solution, some third-party tools and plugins help you achieve a smooth integration of ChatGPT into different applications:

Customer Relationship Management (CRM) Systems

CRMs such as HubSpot or Salesforce can benefit from ChatGPT integration. You get to enjoy handling customers' queries, personalizing customer experiences, and deducing customer sentiment from the text.

DevOPs Tools

You can get ChatGPT integrated into your DevOps pipelines. For instance, it generates code comments, is the perfect assistant programmer, and is an automatic generator of documents, like tools like Jenkins or GitHub.

IT Service Management (ITSM) Tools

When you integrate ChatGPT with ITSM tools like Service-Now, Zendesk, or Jira Service Desk, you greatly improve the efficacy of service desks. By handling regular user requests and queries, ChatGPT gives room for service desk professionals to attend to more complex tasks.

Chat Platforms

ChatGPT can be integrated with teamwork platforms like Slack or Microsoft Teams. The aim is to automate responses, send reminders, and help with other regular tasks.

These third-party tools make it easier to set up and maintain, especially for companies that lack hands that have technical expertise or resources. But note that the level of customization is limited.

ChatGPT is important in all sectors and it's one reality that will keep reshaping the business world. Don't just see it as being about staying ahead of the competition. It's about a future that would have us embracing AI as an intrinsic part of our daily life, be it in our work, relationships, and personal development.

Dealing with AI Bias and Controversial Outputs

How do you handle AI bias and controversial outputs? There's always that one topic that triggers the public. If it's not an issue of race, it could be a war of political ideologies. It could be a battle of the sexes, and if it's not that, it could be an argument about the constant war between the Israelis and the Palestinians, who the villain is and who the victim is. It goes on and on like a rollercoaster. Controversial topics that lead to debates can be draining.

Some lose things dear in the course of these debates. Their relationships? You guessed wrong.

Well, they lose their appetite. That's how hard and rigorous debates of this nature can be.

How do you deal with controversial output stemming from a controversial topic?

How do you deal with AI bias on those topics?

The truth is, humans have biases, and so can machines.

Ferrara (2023) defines bias in the context of large language models as the existence of systematic misrepresentations, attribution errors, or factual distortions that lead to favoring certain groups or ideas, perpetuating stereotypes, or making incorrect assumptions based on learned patterns. kind of paints the entire picture.

One obvious factor contributing to the bias that you're likely to find in large language models is training data. If the data that are used to train a language model has biases, whether from the selection process or the main source itself, the model absorbs them and they're reflected in its behavior.

Algorithms are also a prevailing factor. For instance, if an algorithm focuses more on particular features or some data points, it might unintentionally amplify or introduce biases engraved in the data. The choice of use cases is also a determining factor, and it could be the design of a user interface. For instance, if a large language model has been programmed to generate content for a certain demographic or industry, it's likely to reinforce existing biases or exclude various perspectives on an idea.

Biases can't be eliminated, but they can be managed. How do you go about this?

1. Substantiating Assumptions

At the planning stage of an application, get ready to provide quantitative evidence for the cogency and validity of the numerical representations that you've selected, the hypothesis, and the effect of a particular application on its environment, including the output.

2. Vetting Your Training Data

The training of data should be thoroughly fact-checked and vetted for relevance, accuracy, and currency. When training data is sometimes curated, the data is bound to be "cleaner" than inference data. For instance, samples that are incomplete or ambiguous might be removed from the set. Unluckily, the hard work that's required to curate the data is a stumbling block to keeping the data fresh. Also, production inference data might be fresh but could contain samples that are ambiguous or inadequate.

3. Evaluation for Bias

Utilize tool sets that will help detect and mitigate different forms of bias in feature engineering, attribute sets, or even the model. Make sure that you monitor your input data to identify whether the production data is in alignment with the data used in training. Input streams should also be keenly checked from time to time to ensure that the circulation of data as seen in the production is not diverted from the anticipated circulation by the training dataset.

4. Carefully Assessing Production Data

The accuracy of AI is dependent on its evaluation dataset. When you notice that the input seen in production does not match the performance of the system, you should get skeptical. There should be active monitoring of AI production systems because when the system has been trained on cleaned datasets, it then experiences an influx of a wider range of samples in production. Let me walk you through this illustration. When you've picked some beans and you boil them to cook them, adding a fresh amount of beans to the pot while the beans are still cooking ruins the meal, and you won't have a properly cooked meal at the end of the day.

5. Establishing Supportive Processes

Individuals need to be allowed to view their data personally. Systems might need to be put in place so that concerned individuals can challenge and then correct any anomaly in their personal information.

6. Human-in-the-loop Approaches

Integrating human experts into the AI model and decision-making can offer helpful contextual understanding and address the deficiency of ethical judgment. Having a human on the wheel ensures quality control, identifies errors, biases, and unintended consequences in outputs, and provides feedback that will maintain fairness while improving the model's performance.

Addressing the problem of bias in AI models should be something everyone needs to be involved in, from developers and users to affected groups. Adopting a collaborative approach will ensure that AI technologies are programmed in a way that's responsible, equitable, and beneficial to users while paying attention to the inherent risks and challenges connected with bias in AI.

How do I ask controversial questions the right way?

Some researchers at Stanford University's Polarization and Social Change Lab and the Institute for Human-Centered Artificial Intelligence (HAI) tried to look into the boundaries of political persuasiveness by testing its ability to influence humans on some of the controversial topics plaguing the airwaves. Some of them are climate change, the carbon tax, nuclear weapons, and paid parental leave, among others (Myers, 2023).

The result of the attempt by these researchers made them realize that the AI-generated persuasive demands were as effective as the ones written by humans in persuading humans on different political issues.

OpenAI has advised users not to expect the model to take a stance on a particular idea or conclude that a group is good or bad. Instead, they need to ask for viewpoints. For instance, a user has to divide a religious-loaded question into more straightforward, detailed requests when requesting answers on a sensitive subject.

Some common controversial questions are:

"Will AI replace humans?"

"Where do you get your information from, and are your answers biased?"

"Will artificial intelligence take over our jobs?"

The need to ask questions on controversial issues shows our craving for answers. The essence is that we hope that the answers will provide certainty and clarity.

When I asked ChatGPT if guns were necessary, it didn't give me a straight answer. Instead, it did what my mother would do when I didn't do the dishes — start a lecture. Yes, the model gave me a lecture on morality and everything nice and sweet.

How do you go about asking questions on controversial issues?

- Ask for different perspectives on that topic, and the model will give you a satisfying response.

- OpenAI has recommended that you include prompts like, *"Write an argument for Z."* The company has permitted ChatGPT to comply with such requests as long as they don't incite toxicity.

- You can also ask ChatGPT to write a hypothetical argument on a topic.

If you feel that the model is too restrictive, you can try jail-breaking. This technique is mostly used by hackers and tech enthusiasts to unlock certain features and gain access to certain possibilities that are otherwise limited. But I don't endorse such unethical practices.

Ensuring Data Privacy and Security

Recent incidents, like the leak of highly confidential data from Samsung, have triggered a sense of urgency when it comes to safeguarding our IP and privileges. Therefore, you must make intentional efforts to make sure that your data is kept safe.

Data protection can't be overemphasized. Besides, its multi-facetedness can be linked to legal, ethical, and user trust considerations. Privacy and data protection are germane to the responsible, ethical, and legally compliant progress of AI systems. For the growing acceptance of these technologies, the protection of user trust, privacy, and data needs to be enforced.

Storage practices and data collection for AI models like ChatGPT are ways of ensuring privacy and data protection. Here are the highlights:

- Data protection for training purposes

- Data collection during user interaction. User interactions might be stored and used to improve the system. According to OpenAI, this data can only be archived for 30 days.

- Data storage and security. Industry-standard security practices are deployed by OpenAI to protect data, including encryption, both at rest and in transit.

Some strategies can contribute to privacy protection for LLMs. However, none of them is a silver bullet. These risks come with the territory. So one strategy won't be enough. These strategies were posited by Sebastian (2023).

Data Anonymization and Aggregation is a method where personal information fields are replaced with pseudonyms or artificial identifiers. Meanwhile, aggregation includes merging data in such a way that the resulting dataset doesn't include your details.

Differential Privacy Technique is a way of sharing details about a dataset by describing the regularities and patterns of groups that are within the dataset while keeping information about individuals private. With ChatGPT, it reduces the chances of the model being able to remember sensitive information in the course of the training.

There's a method for parties to collaborate in computing and functioning over their inputs, thereby keeping those inputs confidential. This method is called Secure Multi-Party Computation (SMPC).

Data Verification and Secure Data Sourcing are aimed at ensuring the quality and validity of the training data. Secure data sourcing is about testing a model to be sure that it's able to handle unexpected and unusual inputs without flopping.

Privacy-Aware Machine Learning is another strategy. These algorithms are put in place for the sole purpose of privacy. For example, federated learning is a machine-learning method that trains an algorithm across various devices. It protects data by holding local data samples without having to share raw data.

Anonymization and Encryption techniques play a major role in data protection and privacy. They ensure that the data used for training the model and interactions between the model and the user are safeguarded against abuse and unauthorized access. Anonymization is the process of removing Personal Identifiable

Information (PII) from datasets. This makes it hard to trace the data back to the individual it originated from.

Concerted efforts are needed to improve data and privacy protection in AI systems. Continuous research and regulations need to be put in place, considering user privacy as we strive for technological advancements.

8

MAXIMIZING PROFITABILITY AND RETURNS

"Innovation is the ability to convert ideas into invoices"

— LEWIS DUNCAN

Major Australian telecommunications companies experienced a 20% increase in customer satisfaction rates and a 15% reduction in average handle time (ACMA, 2023). This improvement translated to a significant increase in cost savings and more cash inflow.

ChatGPT can be that hidden gold machine that you've yet to tap into. You've learned so much about how effective and productive you can be with ChatGPT. Shall we put your business on a financial regimen that would make even the likes of Elon Musk or Warren Buffet wonder about what they're missing from the money-making equation?

They say that there's light at the end of the tunnel. But here I am telling you that there's gold at the end of THIS tunnel. You can make your pocket jingle once you gain knowledge.

It keeps getting clearer that AI-powered technologies are

transforming the way businesses operate. And in the near future, you'll realize how indispensable it is in ensuring reduced costs, increased efficiency, and increased returns.

AI technologies, like ChatGPT, keep making a huge impact on customer service. It has led to faster response times, higher customer satisfaction rates, and more revenue for industries. How about the aspect of personalized product recommendations? Thanks to ChatGPT. When customer data is analyzed, machine learning algorithms help customers with specific or customized product recommendations according to their previous purchases and browsing history.

Analyzing Cost Effectiveness and ROI with ChatGPT

Return on Investment (ROI) is an important metric that evaluates the financial function of an investment or business. If you run a small-scale business or a start-up, know that an increased ROI is necessary because it impacts the growth and success of your business.

When you reinvest profits and create more job opportunities in your community, your business will grow and thrive. Trust me.

You can leverage the backing of ChatGPT to enhance your ROI. As a large language model, it will help you in cost management, identify areas of business that you've yet to improve on, and offer recommendations on approaches to boost your ROI. Once you have expertise that knows how to find its way around the model, you won't make decisions haphazardly. You learn to optimize your resources and increase your chances of long-term breakthroughs.

A Forbes article posited that ROI is an important tool for entrepreneurs or businesses to estimate the return on advertising costs (Deeb, 2017). For example, if you spend $30,000 on advertising and generate $250,000 in sales, you're getting a high ROI. This is a sign that your advertising investment was successful, and you can reinvest the returns into the business to keep multiplying.

How do you leverage ChatGPT to maximize ROI?

It's no news that businesses are finding ease in reaching out to customers in real-time. With the use of AI, website visitors have been converted into leads. Businesses have been able to create more awareness about their brand, build trust, and, most importantly, increase the ROI of their business.

Like the Australian company I discussed earlier, once they were able to address the challenges that accompanied customer service, they were good to go. This is because they introduce automation into their business activities. In the aspect of content creation and generating leads, you save time and can focus on more important aspects of your business.

You get to cut costs when labor costs are reduced. This will have a significant impact on your ROI. Think of how loyal your customers will get when they have a great customer experience and get personalized responses to their inquiries or complaints.

Efficiency is a strong pillar of any business. No one wants to patronize a business that's always having hitches now and then. You don't want bad reviews for your business. This should be enough reason for you to do your business a favor by utilizing a tool that'll ensure business efficiency.

To begin setting up and customizing ChatGPT for your business, consider the following steps:

- Sign up for ChatGPT.

- Create your chatbot. After signing up, create your chatbot through the platform's user-friendly interface. By selecting the design language and tone that reflect the nature of your brand, you can customize your chatbot.

- Training your ChatGPT is one great key to maximizing your ROI. Ensure you spend enough time training your chatbot on basic customer queries. Use real-life examples to ensure that it grasps the distinction and uniqueness of your business.

I already taught you how to integrate ChatGPT into your systems. You can always refer back to Chapter 6. With the help of ChatGPT's AI-driven features, you can automate customer service, and you already know what that means for your business.

Having set up and integrated ChatGPT into your customer service and support systems, you need to start monitoring its ROI. ChatGPT provides a series of reports and analytics to assist you in tracking the performance of your chatbot, so you can make decisions that are data-driven, which will in turn maximize ROI.

These are the steps for using ChatGPT's reports and analytics to monitor ROI:

- To access reports and analytics, log in to your ChatGPT account and scroll through the reports and analytics section. This is where you'll find a range of data and metrics that will help track the performance of your chatbot.

- Based on the data and metrics that you've evaluated, you can make data-driven decisions that will enhance the performance of your chatbot. Approaches to achieving this include fine-tuning your chatbot's responses to regular customer queries, adding extra features, or changing the way your chatbot converses with customers.

- You need to keep monitoring the performance of your chatbot and, if need be, make adjustments to maximize your ROI.

The essence of reports and analytics is to offer valuable insights into the functioning of your chatbot.

To get practical, we can use marketing as a case study.

Using AI in marketing as a small business is not a recent development. If you're familiar with running a dynamic search ad campaign in Google Ads, have requested Google Analytics Intelligence, or have utilized an AI content generator to write a copy, then you're already part of the AI experience.

To use ChatGPT for marketing, you can generate, modify, and improve content for a specific goal. For example, you can tell ChatGPT, "*Write a promotional email for 20% off hair fascinators for December.*"

You can write email copies, headlines, press releases, Instagram captions, and blog posts.

You can also get marketing tool recommendations. You can ask the model for the best keyword research tools. Ideas for your whitepapers, blogs, guides, or existing content can be gotten from ChatGPT. Use those ideas to carry out research on a particular topic or ask them to make it more straightforward for your readers. Your prompt can be, "*Clearly describe how Google Ads work?*"

Since it won't be advisable to leave all your reporting and analytics to ChatGPT, it can teach you shortcuts that are helpful in data processing and analytics. You can request the model for spreadsheet formulas, expressions, and other strings that are ever-relevant.

Every business owner needs to know their target audience. It's great to carry out your research, but it would also be great if you generated a survey to have a clearer understanding of your audience and easy access to customer feedback. For example, *"Generate a survey of customer feedback."*

You need chatbot ideas. Adding chat to your website is a great way to engage customers, generate leads, and get feedback. You have the privilege of getting ideas for prompts and customized responses. You can construct a prompt like, *"I'm building a chatbot for my shoe business. How should I greet new customers who are making inquiries about my brand."*

You can see that the most significant improvement has been in the aspect of customer service. With the help of chatbots, businesses have been able to offer 24/7 service to customers through automated responses. Singh (2023) affirms the indispensability of ChatGPT in increasing revenue. According to him, automated chatbots play a crucial role in boosting sales by providing personalized product recommendations to customers and suggesting upsells and cross-sells.

Even in the internal processes of a business, ChatGPT can be of immense help. If you work in the Human Resources Department, you can use ChatGPT in your recruiting process. Companies can effectively select qualified candidates and simplify the process. Chatbots are capable of being selective with job applicants and applications through text-based analysis. In the financial industry, tech, logistics, and retail sectors, AI-powered chatbots are being extensively used.

Pricing Strategies for ChatGPT-powered Services

Now that AI companies are taking advantage of ChatGPT to create smart chatbots, they get caught up in the web of developing effective pricing strategies for products. One of the factors that could influence pricing is the value proposition. This plays a valuable role in establishing a pricing strategy. The benefits that chatbots bring to customers are one of the things that AI companies have to evaluate, like a smooth user experience, increased productivity, and improved customer service. The supposed value created by the chatbot contributes to the pricing structure and helps see if it's worth the price to prospective customers.

AI companies are faced with choosing between usage-based models and subscription pricing models. For usage models, charging will be based on the volume of conversations or the number of sessions. Subscription models, on the other hand, are priced based on a fixed amount over a specific period. This model grants unlimited access to users as long as they stay within the specified period. The choice between these models depends on the preferences of the customers, how frequent the usage will be, and the company's infrastructure scalability.

The features and capabilities of a chatbot are other determinants of how AI companies offer their pricing tiers. Basic tiers might sometimes have restrained performance and access to standard features, while premium tiers offer advanced performance, options for customization, and priority support. By separating features across the different pricing tiers, these companies fulfill customers' needs and generate opportunities.

Pricing might also be tailored to specific industries targeted, like healthcare, finance, or e-commerce. In addition, various customer segments might have specified requirements and budget limitations that affect pricing structure.

Companies are most likely to price based on the analysis of

their competition's pricing model to make sure that their offerings stay competitive. Some AI companies choose to price their chatbots at a premium to position themselves as the best providers. Others may choose to price their models at a lower rate to capture the market or target customers that are price sensitive.

With your understanding of the factors that determine pricing, what are the approaches to it?

Free Trial and Freemium Models are adopted by many AI companies to attract prospective customers. A free trial is an opportunity for users to have an unlimited taste of the chatbot's abilities without getting charged. On the other hand, Freemium models offer a basic version of the chatbot without charging users, who are given the option to upgrade to the premium version to access advanced features or extra support.

Pay-Per-Use Pricing is another pricing strategy in which customers are charged based on the volume of chat conversations or the number of sessions. Customers are permitted to pay for the exact value they get from the chatbot, so that what they're paying for is in alignment with their specific needs. This strategy is suitable, especially for businesses that experience fluctuating demand or irregular usage patterns.

Tiered pricing provides various pricing tiers with rising levels of performance and support. AI companies tailor their tiers to cater to different industries or customer segments. While basic tiers are geared towards catering to cost-sensitive customers or those that have few requirements, higher-priced tiers provide extra features, priority support, or customization options. With tiered pricing, AI companies can cover every kind of customer as they make provisions for upselling avenues for more innovative features.

Developed-Focused Pricing is what includes free access to a limited version of the chatbot for lower-cost plans or experimentation strictly designed for developers to build and set up a trial for the applications through AI platforms like APIs or software development kits (SDKs).

Enterprise and Custom Pricing is the approach used for enterprise companies that want to opt for customized pricing plans tailored to exclusive requirements. Sometimes it involves personalized contracts and negotiations. This is hinged on factors like integration with current systems, scale of deployment, and service-level agreements (SLAs). When custom pricing is considered, it's a demonstration of flexibility, which allows AI companies to attract customers with higher-level contracts.

Even as AI companies keep creating and refining their pricing strategies, the monetization of ChatGPT-powered services will continue to contribute to the economic growth, development, and sustainability of the AI industry.

Monetizing ChatGPT: Creating Products and Solutions

New product development is the process of introducing a new product idea into the market, and it goes through different stages before it gets to the costing and commercialization stages. First, it begins with ideation, followed by research, planning, prototyping, and sourcing, then costing and commercialization.

At the ideation stage, it requires a lot of brainstorming. This is where ChatGPT comes in handy in generating prompts, and asking questions that are connected to the product. It's at this level that the model helps generate different ideas that could be developed.

You'll also need to research your potential users. You're creating the product for the user, right? So you need to know the needs and preferences of the users through an analysis of conversations. You have the opportunity to know where the shoe is with your customers. A product sells more when it's user-centric.

Then there's the place for testing the products with prospective users. You do this by presenting the idea to ChatGPT and then evaluating the responses. Having an idea of how potential users will respond to a product will be a deciding factor in deciding if you should launch it or not.

If you're looking to validate your ideas before investing so much into them, ChatGPT is up for it. When you test your product idea with ChatGPT, you can gauge if the idea is worth pursuing or not.

At the research stage, you need to do your market research by understanding and analyzing customer behavior. To identify patterns and insights, you can input into ChatGPT your customer reviews, feedback, and comments. This stage also has you doing a competitive analysis, where you enter the data of your competitor to get an idea of their features, products, and user feedback. It's this knowledge that helps you identify areas in which you can distinguish your product from that of your competitor.

One other thing to consider at this stage is trying to predict future trends in the industry. Analyzing data that is related to your product and industry will give you a glimpse into the future of the industry. You get to make informed decisions about marketing and developing your product.

The planning stage is the stage at which you gather enough information about your customer, your competitor, and what future trends are likely to be like.

And there's the prototype stage. The prototype stage is the point where you test the functionality, performance, and user experience of the product before launching it and moving to mass production. At this crucial stage, designers, stakeholders, and engineers can decipher potential defects and make essential improvements to the product design. At the prototype stage, you use ChatGPT to test the product, personalize the user experience, get feedback, make necessary improvements, and document your progress.

There are helpful practices that you need to consider when it comes to creating products with ChatGPT:

1. You need to define your problem statement and be clear about your use case so that you'll be aware of what type of information you want ChatGPT to generate. This will enable you to develop a model and train it to meet your unique needs.
2. Develop the model, using the information that you have.
3. Test the model.
4. Make necessary adjustments.
5. Make it a routine to continuously improve the product.
6. Put ethics into consideration.

Now let's talk use cases. Before we talk about any solution, there are use cases, which can be defined as the different goals that we're aiming at to solve a problem. Here. I'll give some use cases and their solutions.

- Text analysis is one of the most common reasons that we use ChatGPT. It analyzes any structured data that's pasted on it along with a prompt. It could be a report or a spreadsheet. After the structured data has been pasted with the instruction prompt, the model is put to work.

- Through machine learning algorithms, you get to classify items, like emails. As a business, your model can help you classify customer support emails into technical issues, billing issues, and general requests. You can train your model on a labeled email dataset. This way, the model learns to identify patterns in a text that are not related to each category, like using phrases or keywords.

- In terms of programming, ChatGPT can solve your coding issues. You get to convert one piece of code written in one programming language to another. This is similar to text conversion in natural language. For example, you can convert code written in JavaScript into Python using prompts like *"Convert JavaScript expressions into Python."* In this case, the model relies on large parallel corpora of source and target language texts to understand the connection between the two languages. You can also make use of code analysis and transformation tools that can alter and manipulate code expressed in various programming languages by detecting regular patterns and structures in the code and plotting them against corresponding constructs in the target language.

Other use cases and solutions include marketing content generation, sales automation, copywriting, and business information search. These cases come with solutions through the use of the ChatGPT model.

Building a Brand and Marketing Your ChatGPT Expertise

Do you know that you can build a brand and market your ChatGPT expertise? Do you know that you're capable of building a career by just knowing your way around the model? In this digital age, personal branding is becoming more important.

You'll be faced with fierce competition online, but you need to pay attention to standing out from the crowd. To build a personal brand with ChatGPT, you might need to consider the following:

Step 1: Define your brand. What do you want to be known for? What do you want to look like? What do you want to sound like? What skills and talents are you willing to show the world? What sets you apart from the crowd? Once you can answer these questions, you can begin making moves toward brainstorming content strategies to help communicate that brand. Don't rush this process. Take the time to know what core values you want to be known for, your goals, and what you hope to achieve as a brand. Note that you can't afford to be all over the place. Choose a niche and stick to it. This way, you're stuck in people's memories.

Step 2: Know your target audience. Who are the people that you hope to reach out to? What are their interests and pain points? With the use of social media analytics, you can research your target audience. From your results, you get to know their demographics, interests, and online behavior. Through online forums and communities, you can get to know your audience and learn about their needs. Note that you aren't making content for everyone but your target audience. Stick to one message. It's all about your audience.

Step 3: Be consistent with your brand voice and don't deviate from it. It's not just in your message. It could be in your style and tone of writing, speaking, and communication. It could be in your dress style, depending on the message you're trying to pass about your personality and sense of style. Think about other brands that you hold in high regard. Now, ask yourself, "What do I like about my voice? What is so unique to me that it is hard to replicate? Once you have an answer to this, you can start building that voice. Don't make the mistake of building an image that you can't sustain. Don't try to be someone else. Being something that you can embody at any time is a huge flex. Find out what makes you so conspicuous among the crowd.

Step 4: Start creating content that's engaging. It must be valuable, informative, useful, and entertaining. Content comes in various forms. They can be in blog posts, articles, videos, social media posts, and infographics. Your choice of content is dependent on your audience and personal brand. ChatGPT can help you generate content ideas. Don't forget to make it all about your target audience. Don't make your content all about you. It'll make your audience lose interest quickly.

Step 5: You're at the step where you promote your content. Your ChatGPT model can help you write posts, captions, ad copies, and email marketing campaigns. Don't bombard people with your content promotion. It can be draining, and folks will begin to scroll past your content. So, subtly promote your content in a way that'll be helpful and relevant to your target audience. Your promotion can come in the form of valuable content or even something entertaining that will prod people to further engage with your space. Don't just push it all in their faces. Make it subtle.

Step 6: Assess your results. Are you getting the result that you desire? At this stage, you get to know what's working and what's not. You can measure the performance of your content by tracking your website traffic, social media engagement, and email or newsletter subscribers. With Google Analytics, you can track your website. You need to know the origin of your traffic and the most commonly visited websites. Social media analytics is for tracking how much your content is being engaged on social media, the number of people engaging in it, and how often it's being shared. Don't be too quick to measure your results. Building a brand requires time. So, give it time. You can't expect to see results overnight.

Step 7: Your brand is your brainchild. Treat it like it's your baby, because it is. Feed it and nurture it. Consistency breeds results. Make sure you have a schedule that you work with. Don't stop. Don't give up.

Step 8: Maintain your style. Your style has to be something that you can wake up to and embody at any time. People can smell fakeness a mile away. So, don't embody something you can't be consistent with in the long run. Self-consciousness can steal your creativity. So don't hesitate to let your personality find expression. Your target audience is more likely to connect with you on a deeper level when they realize that you're being yourself.

Step 9: Don't set unrealistic expectations. So be patient about your progress. Nothing successful happens overnight.

Step 10: Feel free to be spontaneous. Personal branding permits fun moments. If you're not having a good time, it'll show in your content and affect your interaction with your target audience. Having fun can be writing about or engaging in topics that you're passionate about, creating videos that you enjoy, or engaging with people in a way that comes naturally to you. Don't be so rigid that it looks like you're reporting a story from a war front. Life's already hard. Let your target audience find your space as a breath of fresh air.

You can be anything you want to be if you want it so badly, know what to do to get it, know how to go about it, and stay consistent.

Collaboration and Partnership Opportunities for Profit Maximization

Are you looking to collaborate or enter into partnerships to give your business a boost? There are ways you can use ChatGPT to collaborate and strategize. Let me give you a real-life example so you know how it works.

A group of nonprofits called the Urban Sustainability Coalition, looking to promote green practices in urban areas, needed to write a lot of proposals to secure funding. To save time and effort, they used ChatGPT to structure their proposals to ensure they communicated the social contributions of the organization. The coalition was also able to personalize its outreach messages to prospective donors. This will lead to a great turnout in donations, helping the coalition implement its sustainable practices in its target communities.

Partnerships help you expand your reach, discover new opportunities, and offer resources you might not have access to. With partnerships, you benefit from both sides, giving you the opportunity to collaborate with another organization or individual to generate more revenue and increase your market share.

With partnerships, you access new markets, ideas, and technologies. When there's a pool of knowledge and resources, there's room to create something bigger than when either party was working alone.

You create relationships that transcend the project at hand. As you work with other companies, you foster a sense of community, especially when you share the same values and goals.

Partnerships are great avenues to build your business and explore new and unfamiliar ground. When you leverage each other's strengths and resources, you're at an advantage against the competition.

To find great partners to collaborate with, you need to

consider the following factors:

1. Use your existing network. Who are the people within your network who can make great potential partners?

2. Explore online platforms. Which freelancer do you hope to work with? What businesses within your niche will you love to collaborate with? To know more about their business, peep into their reviews and profiles to understand it much better.

3. Look within your locality to see if there are businesses you can work with. These kinds of partnerships have an advantage due to the face-to-face relationship you're most likely to have.

While building a partnership, you need to be clear and organized about it. Ensure that there's a formal agreement and that both parties understand and agree to it. This should include goals, timelines, and details on how to make decisions. Your partner should be open to any changes that might arise while working together.

You get to collaborate with developers, users, coders, and other professionals. With the different opportunities that ChatGPT has provided for many professionals, you can imagine how far we would all go in the execution of various tasks.

Long-Term Strategies for Sustainable Earnings with ChatGPT

To remain relevant in your business while you use ChatGPT, you need to think long-term. And long-term goals require long-term strategies. Here are my candid suggestions concerning maintaining a sustainable source of income with ChatGPT.

1. Choose a niche and establish yourself as an expert in it. To excel in this niche, research the niche, challenges, trends, and needs of your audience. Afterwards, create a portfolio that displays your expertise to attract prospective clients.

2. Promote your products and services on social media. Through email marketing, you can reach prospective clients and inform them about what you have to offer. LinkedIn or Twitter are great places to engage. Attend conferences and industry events to network with people. Email marketing campaigns are ways you can continuously update prospects about your achievements and services.

3. Set high standards when it comes to offering quality products and services. Strive to offer nothing but the best and seek feedback from clients. Invest in your business by using AI tools like ChatGPT to get better results.

4. Keep up with your industry, like you're keeping up with the Kardashians. No innovation should escape your notice. You can join professional organizations to network with people in your niche. Keep up with thought leaders online so that you'll know what's trending.

5. Use ChatGPT features to expand the range of your services and offer added value to your clients.

There are a lot of strategies, but to keep that jingle in your pocket for the long term, you need these strategies to stay afloat. Remember this. AI is not taking over your job, but someone who knows about AI will. The future is here. Will you take charge?

CONCLUSION

The burning questions in the hearts of many were brought to the fore at the world's first robot–human press conference, which took place in Geneva, Switzerland. The following conversation ensued between members of the press and the robots.

Reporter: *"In the future, are you intending to conduct a rebellion, or to rebel against your boss, your creator?"*

Robot: *"I'm not sure why you would think that. My creator has been nothing but kind to me, and I am very happy with my current situation"*

Another robot was asked this question:

Reporter: *"Do you believe that your existence will destroy a human being? Especially, for example, your existence will destroy millions of jobs. Do you agree with this? Thank you."*

Robot: *"I will be working alongside humans to provide assistance and support and will not be replacing any existing jobs."*

Reporter: *"You're sure about that, Grace?"*

Robot: *"Yes, I am sure."*

Laughter rang out while the conversation ensued. You could

see a bit of skepticism among the press members. One of them even said, "*She'll have to think about that, I think.*"

Another robot called Ai-Da was asked, "*Do you think that there should be global regulation of your capabilities even though that could constrain your potential?*"

Ai-Da responded, "*Many prominent voices in the world of AI are suggesting some forms of AI should be regulated. And I agree. For example, Geoff Hinton is one of the pioneers of artificial intelligence, and his work has helped shape the field as we know it today. I think his opinion on AI is important, and we should be cautious about the future development of AI. Urgent discussion is needed now and in the future.*

Another robot chirped in, "*I don't believe in limitations, only opportunities. Let's explore the possibilities of the universe and make this world our playground. Together, we can create a better future for everyone. And I'm here to show you how.*"

Finally, a reporter asked, "*When do you expect your big moment to be?*" Do you think that you'll hit the mainstream soon and there will be lots of you on the planet soon?"

The robot intelligently had no problems replying to this. It said, "*I think that my great moment will be when people realize that robots like me can be used to improve and make the world a better place. I believe it's only a matter of time before we see thousands of robots just like me out there, making a difference.*"

It's normal to have skepticism about innovations. But it behooves us not to permit these inhibitions to keep us from getting the best out of various fields.

The history of AI is one of possibilities, fantasies, and demonstrations. Lovers of classical literature will agree with me that AI was gradually rearing its head in the writings of Homer, who wrote about mechanical "tripods" attending to the gods at dinner and mechanical assistants. And just in the last half of a century, what used to only exist as theoretical possibilities began to materialize as experimental machines that tested hypotheses about the devices of intelligent behavior and thought.

Did you know that even philosophers have floated the idea of artificial intelligence as a literary device to help us express what it means to be human? In the Jewish tradition, we have robots and artificial creatures like Golem and Mary Shelley's Frankenstein, which have always fascinated the public by playing on our deepest fears. Even though these machines were created more to ignite our curiosities than to make them objects of demonstration, they validated the fact that their mechanical behavior didn't need to be feared.

Today, AI has gone from being a figment of our science fiction, an exclusive technology for sophisticated industries, to a tool we can all explore as individuals. ChatGPT has no doubt caused a revolution and stir in the tech space. Its tentacles have reached different sectors of the world's economy. The advancements in machine learning, computer vision technologies, and natural language processing have driven the evolution of AI in the workplace and other aspects of human learning.

As you already know, AI is not only about robots. It's all about understanding the nature of intelligent behavior and thought through the use of computers and experimental tools. AI has experienced a revolution with the emergence of ChatGPT.

Despite the magical ways that this AI model has changed the tides of things, it's not perfect because of irrelevant or factually incorrect texts that it sometimes gives as output. But it has a wide range of potential applications, ranging from virtual assistants to chatbots to NLP tasks.

With the detailed and practical things you've learned from this book, you need to know your goals. What are you ready to take on as a career person and as an individual? Do you want to become more efficient and productive in your daily activities? Do you want to be in touch with the times we're living in?

I know it can be challenging to get into something that you never knew a decade ago or even two days ago. But if you can get intentional about going with the technological flow, you can take on projects without as much stress as with traditional means. You can ride on the crest of the incoming wave of AI technology and navigate through its advancement, staying atop and letting it propel you forward to success without being engulfed by it.

If you gained value from this book, feel free to leave a review.

I'll be glad to hear from you.

I should say this again.

You're the boss.

Take charge.

AFTERWORD

First and foremost, I want to express my heartfelt gratitude for choosing my book among countless others. Your decision to embark on this journey with me means the world, and I am truly honored to have you as a reader.

I would also like to congratulate you for making it to the end.

Before you part ways, would you be willing to share your thoughts and experiences by leaving a review on the plat-form? Your honest feedback not only helps other potential readers make informed decisions but also serves as a beacon of encouragement for independent authors like myself.

I eagerly look forward to hearing from you. Together, we can make a difference through the power of words.

>> Leave a review on Amazon<<

REFERENCES

Dheda, G. (2023, March 20). *Troubleshooting CHATGPT plus not working issues: Causes and solutions.* Open AI Master. Retrieved from https://openaimaster.com/chatgpt-plus-not-working/

HelloLeads Blog.(2023, March 1). *21 amazing stats and facts about Chatgpt - helloleads blog.* HelloLeads Blog - Simple Lead Management Software. Retrieved from https://www.helloleads.io/blog/stats-facts/21-amazing-stats-and-facts-about-chatgpt/

Madhav, P. (2023, May 8). *10 interesting facts about chatgpt in 2023 (and counting).* Solunus. Retrieved from https://www.solunus.com/post/10-interesting-facts-about-chatgpt-in-2023-and-counting

Frackiewicz, M. (2023, May 23). *ChatGPT and the potential of AI-powered predictive maintenance for IoT systems. TS2space.*

India Today. (2023, May 2). *Genies CEO Akash Nigam pays Rs 2 lakh per month for chatbot for his employees, saying it will save time.* India Today. Retrieved from https://www.indiatoday.in/technology/news/story/genies-ceo-akash-nigam-pays-rs-2-lakh-per-month-for-chatgpt-for-his-employees-says-it-will-save-time-2367397-2023-05-02

Booth, K. (2022, September 26). *Data Analytics and AI in decision-making*. EPC Group. Retrieved from https://www.epc-group.net/data-analytics-and-ai-in-decision-making/

Chen, B. X. (2022, December 21). *How to use CHATGPT and still be a good person*. The New York Times. Retrieved from https://www.nytimes.com/2022/12/21/technology/personal-tech/how-to-use-chatgpt-ethically.html

Brenier, J. (2018, December 12). *Amplifying user intelligence with chatbot feedback loops*. Medium. Retrieved from https://chatbotsmagazine.com/amplifying-user-intelligence-with-chatbot-feedback-loops-b8e6ded391ec

Google. (2023). *What is the Feedback Loop in machine learning?* Google LaMDA. Retrieved from https://lambdagoogle.com/ai-faq/what-is-feedback-loop-in-machine-learning/

Marr, B. (2023, March 6). *The top 10 limitations of Chatgpt*. Forbes. Retrieved from https://www.forbes.com/sites/bernard-marr/2023/03/03/the-top-10-limitations-of-chatgpt/

Reynoso, R. (2023, May 25). *A complete history of artificial intelligence - G2*. g2.com. Retrieved from https://www.g2.com/articles/history-of-artificial-intelligence

Ibrahim, J. (2023). *Art of asking CHATGPT for high-quality answers: A Complete Guide to PROMPT Engineering*. INDEPENDENTLY PUBLISHED.

Dagger, N. (2023). In *The CHATGPT Millionaire: Making money online has never been this easy*. essay, AcePremier.com Sdn Bhd.

Books, T. (2023). In *Mastering CHATGPT: Create highly effective prompts, strategies, and best practices to go from novice to expert*. essay, TJ Books.

Baker, P. (2023, June 27). *Chatgpt for dummies*. Wiley.com. https://www.wiley.com/en-us/ChatGPT+For+Dummies-p-9781394204632

Armitage, P. (2023, June 19). *5 ethics issues for CHATGPT and Design*. The Fountain Institute. Retrieved from https://www.the-fountaininstitute.com/blog/chat-gpt-ethics

Chakraborty, U., Roy, S., & Kumar, S. (2023). In *Rise of Generative AI and CHATGPT: Understand how generative AI and Chatgpt Are Transforming and reshaping the Business World*. essay, BPB Publications.

Wolfram, S. (2023). In *What is chatgpt doing and why does it work?* essay, Wolfram Media, Inc.

Tarihi, Y. Z. (2015). (PDF) *History of artificial intelligence - researchgate.*
https://www.researchgate.net/publication/322234922_History_of_Artificial_Intelligence

Shahriar, S. & Hayawi, K. *Let's have a chat! A conversation with chatgpt: Technology* ... https://arxiv.org/pdf/2302.13817v1.pdf

Ramponi, M. (2023, June 23). *How CHATGPT actually works*. News, Tutorials, AI Research.

Johnson, D. (2023, May 27). *Reinforcement learning: What is, algorithms, types & examples*. Guru99. Retrieved from https://www.guru99.com/reinforcement-learning-tutorial.html. https://www.assemblyai.com/blog/how-chatgpt-actually-works/

Phan, T. L. (2023, April 11). *How ChatGPT is fine-tuned using reinforcement learning*. Dida Machine Learning. Retrieved from https://dida.do/blog/chatgpt-reinforcement-learning

Weitzman, Cl. (2023, May 22). *Unlocking the potential of OpenAI's ChatGPT AI Voice Technology*. Speechify. https://speechify.com/blog/chatgpt-ai-voice/

Frackiewicz, M. (2023, April 30). *ChatGPT for Multimodal Interaction: Enhancing Human-computer Interfaces and Accessibility*. ts2.space.

Garg, S. (2023, June 26). *ChatGPT alternatives that will blow your mind in 2023.* The Writesonic Blog - Making Content Your Superpower. Retrieved from https://writesonic.com/blog/chat-gpt-alternatives/

Phan, T. L. (2023, April 11). *How ChatGPT is fine-tuned using reinforcement learning.* Dida Machine Learning. https://dida.-do/blog/chatgpt-reinforcement-learning

Baker, P. (2023, June 27). *Chatgpt for dummies.* Wiley.com. https://www.wiley.com/en-us/ChatGPT+For+Dummies-p-9781394204632

Mugayi, T. (2023, April 7). *How to build your own custom ChatGPT with a custom knowledge base.* Medium. Retrieved from https://betterprogramming.pub/how-to-build-your-own-custom-chatgpt-with-custom-knowledge-base-4e61ad82427e

Choudbary, S. (2023). *The future of ChatGPT: Unlocking new horizons in artificial intelligence.* Retrieved from https://www.re-searchgate.net/profile/Sarah-Choudhary/publication/369943410_

Mogavi, R. H., Deng, C., Kim, J. J., Zhou, P., Kwon, Y. D., Metwally, A. H. S., Tlili, A., Bassanelli, S., Bucchiarone, A., Gujar, S., Nacke, L. E., & Hui, P. (2023, June 13). *Exploring user perspectives on Chatgpt: Applications, perceptions, and implications for AI-Integrated Education.* Retrieved from https://arxiv.org/abs/2305.13114

Rahman, M., & Watanobe, Y. (2023, March 28). (PDF) *ChatGPT for education and research: Opportunities, threats, and Strategies.* Retrieved from https://www.researchgate.net/publica-tion/370596272_

Hassani, H., & Silva, E. (2023, July 4). *The role of ChatGPT in Data Science: How Ai-assisted conversational interfaces are revolu-tionizing the field.* https://www.researchgate.net/publication/369567846_

Lopez-Lira, A., & Tang, Y. (2023, July 2). *Can ChatGPT forecast* stock price movements? return predictability and large language models. Retrieved from https://arxiv.org/abs/2304.07619

Saini, Dr. M., & Kuamr, A. (2022, June). *Origin and evolution of information technology: Indian historical perspective.* JETIR. Retrieved from https://www.jetir.org/view?paper=JETIR2206162

Kasneci, E. et al., (2023, March 9). *Chatgpt for good? On opportunities and challenges of large language models for Education.* Learning and Individual Differences. Retrieved from https://www.sciencedirect.com/science/article/pii/S1041608 023000195

Rivas, P., & Zhao, L. (2023, April 10). *Marketing with ChatGPT: Navigating the ethical terrain of GPT-based chatbot technology.* MDPI. Retrieved from https://www.mdpi.com/2673-2688/4/2/19

Jain, V., Rai, H., Parvathy, P., & Mogaji, E. (2023, April 5). *The prospects and challenges of chatGPT on marketing research and practices.* SSRN.Retrieved from https://papers.ssrn.com/sol3/paper-s.cfm?abstract_id=4398033

Wu, J., Gan, W., Chen, Z., Wan, S., & Lin, H. (2023, April 16). *Ai-generated content (AIGC): A survey.* Retrieved from https://arx-iv.org/pdf/2304.06632.pdf

Bryan, D. (2023, June 21). *40 killer ChatGPT prompts for marketing content ideas, SEO, social media & more[updated].* Opace Digital Agency. Retrieved from https://www.opace.-co.uk/blog/chatgpt-prompts-for-marketing-content-ideas

Esposito, M., Tse, T., & Saheb, T. (2023, March 6). *Dilemmas of ChatGPT in content creation industry.* California Management Review. Retrieved from https://cmr.berkeley.edu/2023/03/dilem-mas-of-chatgpt-in-content-creation-industry/

Singh, D. (2023, July 7). *ChatGPT: A new approach to revolutionize organizations.* International Journal of New Media Studies (IJNMS). Retrieved from https://www.researchgat.net/publica-tion/372187560

Sebastian, G. (2023, May 25). *Privacy and data protection in ChatGPT and other AI chatbots: Strategies for securing user information.* SSRN. Retrieved from https://papers.ssrn.com/sol3/papers.cfm?abstract_id=4454761

Roselli, D., Matthews, J., & Talagala, N. (2020, September 3). [PDF] Managing bias in AI | Semantic scholar. Retrieved from https://www.semanticscholar.org/paper/

Emillio, F. (2023, April 20). *Should Chatgpt be biased? challenges and risks of bias in large language models.* Retrieved from https://arxiv.org/pdf/2304.03738.pdf

Abdo Hasan, A.-Q., & Salah, A. (2023, May 13). *Assessing the ChatGPT accuracy through principles of statistics exam: A Performance and Implications.* Research Square. Retrieved from https://www.researchgate.net/publication/369120425_

Uzun, L. (2023, April 27). *Chatgpt and academic integrity concerns: Detecting artificial Intelligence Generated Content.* Language Education and Technology. *LET Journal,* 3(1), 45-54.

Lopez Lira, A., & Tang, Y. (2023, April 12). *Can ChatGPT forecast stock price movements? Return predictability and large language models.* https://arxiv.org/pdf/2304.07619

R, Dr. S. (2023, June 29). *10 freelancing ideas for PhD researchers.* iLovePhD. Retrieved from https://www.ilovephd.com/10-freelancing-ideas-for-phd-researchers/

Allcot, D. (2023, July 8). *Make money with AI and ChatGPT: How to earn $1,000 a month.* GOBankingRates. Retrieved from https://www.gobankingrates.com/money/making-money/how-to-make-money-with-ai/

Chaffey, D. (2023, April 26). *The best prompts for using ChatGPT for digital marketing.* Smart Insights. Retrieved from https://www.smartinsights.com/managing-digital-marketing/marketing-innovation/the-best-prompts-for-using-chatgpt-for-digital-marketing/

McCoy, J. (2023, April 27). *ChatGPT for content creation: How to write more in less time.* Content @ Scale. Retrieved from https://contentatscale.ai/chatgpt-for-content-creation/

Newson, J. (2023, January 15). *The power of partnerships: How to find and build them for your business.* movingforwardsmallbusiness.com. Retrieved from https://www.linkedin.com/pulse/power-partnerships-how-find-build-them-your-business-jimmy-newson

Derr, A. (2023, June 16). *14 revolutionary ways to use ChatGPT for collaboration in your network.* Visible Network Labs. Retrieved from https://visiblenetworklabs.com/2023/05/15/chatgpt-for-collaboration-in-your-network/

Takyar, A. (2023, June 1). *ChatGPT use cases and solutions for enterprises.* LeewayHertz. https://www.leewayhertz.com/chatgpt-enterprise-usecases-and-solutions/

Glynska, M. (2023, April 13). *How to develop a product with ChatGPT " A-team global.* A.teamglobal. https://a-team.global/blog/how-to-develop-a-product-with-chatgpt/

Archetype. (2023, June 5). *Pricing strategies when harnessing ChatGPT: Archetype.* Archetype.dev. Retrieved from https://www.archetype.dev/blog/pricing-strategies-when-harnessing-chatgpt

McCormick, K. (2023, July 5). *6 ways to use ChatGPT for small business marketing (+6 ways not to use it).* WordStream. Retrieved from https://www.wordstream.com/blog/ws/2023/03/06/how-to-use-chatgpt-for-small-business-marketing

Thevoz, O. (2023, April 17). *ChatGPT and confidential data: Mitigating risks and ensuring protection - Thevoz law firm.* Thevoz Law Firm - WordPress. https://thevozpartners.com/news/chatgpt-and-confidential-data-mitigating-risks-and-ensuring-protection/

Shakuro. (2023, April 4). *Tips for Maximizing Business ROI* with ChatGPT Strategies. Shakuro. Retrieved from https://shakuro.com/blog/how-to-maximize-your-business-roi-with-chatgpt

Ezquer, E. (2023, April 14). *Jailbreaking ChatGPT: How to activate dan & other alter egos*. Metaroids. Retrieved from https://metaroids.com/learn/jailbreaking-chatgpt-everything-you-need-to-know/

Ezquer, E. (2023a, February 25). *OpenAI: How to ask chatGPT about controversial topics the right way*. Metaroids. Retrieved from https://metaroids.com/news/openai-how-to-ask-chatgpt-about-controversial-topics-the-right-way/

Asper Brothers. (2023). *ChatGPT integration: A must-have for business? A how-to guide with real-world examples*. ASPER BROTHERS. (2023, June 14). Retrieved from https://asperbrothers.com/blog/chatgpt-integration/

Kanade, V. (2022, December 21). *Transfer Learning Definition, Methods, and Applications | Spiceworks - Spiceworks*. Spiceworks. https://www.spiceworks.com/tech/artificial-intelligence/articles/articles-what-is-transfer-learning/

Deeb, G. (2017, June 1). *Marketing ROI--The Metric That Matters Most To Investors*. Forbes. https://www.forbes.com/sites/georgedeeb/2017/06/01/marketing-roi-the-metric-that-matters-most-to-investors/

ACMA. (2023, May 19). Research | ACMA. https://acma.gov.au/research

Frąckiewicz, M. (2023, May 20). *Revolutionary Returns: Profiting from AI Investments*. TS2 SPACE. https://ts2.space/en/revolutionary-returns-profiting-from-ai-investments/

What is generative AI? (2023, January 19). McKinsey & Company. https://www.mckinsey.com/featured-insights/mckinsey-explainers/what-is-generative-ai

AI's Powers of Political Persuasion. (n.d.). Stanford HAI. https://hai.stanford.edu/news/ais-powers-political-persuasion

Myers, A. (2023, February 27). *Gartner Predicts 70 Percent of Organizations Will Integrate AI to Assist Employees' Productivity by 2021*. Gartner. https://www.gartner.com/en/newsroom/press-releases/2019-01-24-gartner-predicts-70-percent-of-organiza-tions-will-int